THE SANDARS LECTURES IN BIBLIOGRAPHY

THOMAS HOLLIS
OF LINCOLN'S INN

Thomas Hollis, a connoisseur and collector of art and antiquities, devoted the greater part of his substance and his energy to promoting the ideals of civil and religious liberty. He is best known to modern bibliophiles for the distinctive bindings that he commissioned for the many books he distributed in Britain, the American colonies, and all over Europe. This book contains the first comprehensive catalogue and interpretation of his emblematic binding tools and a discussion of the several binders who worked for him. It also explores other activities that are less well known: his patronage of writers, printers, publishers, and artists, and his work as a designer of books and medals. This study should encourage a re-evaluation of Hollis's influence in the Age of Enlightenment and the Age of Revolution.

T0382594

Crayon drawing of Thomas Hollis by Giovanni Battista
Cipriani, 1767 (detail)

THOMAS HOLLIS
OF LINCOLN'S INN

A WHIG AND HIS BOOKS

W. H. BOND

Librarian Emeritus
The Houghton Library
Harvard University

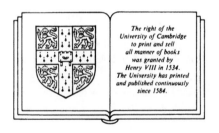

The right of the
University of Cambridge
to print and sell
all manner of books
was granted by
Henry VIII in 1534.
The University has printed
and published continuously
since 1584.

CAMBRIDGE UNIVERSITY PRESS

Cambridge
New York   Port Chester
Melbourne   Sydney

CAMBRIDGE UNIVERSITY PRESS
Cambridge, New York, Melbourne, Madrid, Cape Town, Singapore, São Paulo, Delhi

Cambridge University Press
The Edinburgh Building, Cambridge CB2 8RU, UK

Published in the United States of America by Cambridge University Press, New York

www.cambridge.org
Information on this title: www.cambridge.org/9780521114806

First published 1990
This digitally printed version 2009

A catalogue record for this publication is available from the British Library

Library of Congress Cataloguing in Publication data
Bond, W. H. (William Henry), 1915–
Thomas Hollis of Lincoln's Inn: a Whig and his books / W. H. Bond.
p. cm. – (The Sandars lectures in bibliography)
ISBN 0–521–39091–5
1. Hollis, Thomas, 1720–1774. 2. Hollis, Thomas, 1720–1774 –
Library. 3. Book collectors – Great Britain – Biography. 4. Book
collecting – England – History – 18th century. 5. Bookbinding –
England – History – 18th century. 6. Emblems – England – History – 18th
century. 7. Bibliography – Early printed books. 8. Harvard College
Library. I. Title. II. Series.
Z989.H65B66 1990
381′.45002′074092 – dc20
[B] 89–77370 CIP

ISBN 978-0-521-39091-0 hardback
ISBN 978-0-521-11480-6 paperback

In memory of
four men of books
A. N. L. Munby
Howard M. Nixon
William A. Jackson
Philip Hofer

But if there be in glory aught of good
It may by means far different be attain'd,
Without ambition, war, or violence;
By deeds of peace, by wisdom eminent,
By patience, temperance. . .

John Milton, *Paradise Regained*, III:88–92

Contents

Illustrations

Preface

Thomas Hollis of Lincoln's Inn was regarded by most of his contemporaries as a more or less harmless eccentric, perhaps to be looked upon with some suspicion as an atheist (which he was not) and watched as a radical and potential trouble-maker. They misjudged him. He was, in fact, quietly and vigorously pursuing a course of public service, inspired, as he was in many of his actions, by the writings of his chief literary hero, John Milton. Among many Miltonian writings that shaped his life, the epigraph of this book and the forty-one lines that precede it in *Paradise Regained* are peculiarly significant. 'By deeds of peace' was one of the mottoes most frequently inscribed in the many books that he placed strategically in libraries and in the hands of his contemporaries in Europe and the New World.

In the two centuries since his death, his chief fame among librarians and collectors has arisen from the striking emblematic bindings that he commissioned for those books; still, however, considered as a curiosity. Twentieth-century scholars, led by Professor Chester Noyes Greenough and more recently by Professors Caroline Robbins and John L. Abbott, have penetrated Hollis's self-protective veil of anonymity and have gone far towards establishing him in his rightful position in intellectual and political history. The books he gave away or caused to be reprinted were not random choices, nor were the symbols adorning them; and the web of his personal contacts and correspondence is a significant manifestation of the Enlightenment and the struggle for civil and religious freedom, a struggle by no means at an end even today.

The present study, originally delivered in the spring of 1982 as a series of four lectures while I was Sandars Reader in Bibliography, attempts to carry this work of rehabilitation still further. Lectures such as these are inevitably bounded by constraints imposed by the patience and endurance of the lecturer's audience. The four chapters that follow reflect the four lectures, but each has been revised and to some degree expanded in the light of subsequent research and much correspondence with librarians, collectors, scholars, and book dealers, the extent of which will be readily apparent in my acknowledgements and footnotes.

It is not false modesty to say that some statements uttered in the lectures were mistaken, much was left unsaid not only through lack of time but also through ignorance, and much of interest remains to be discovered about Thomas Hollis. I would be the last to claim that full justice has now been done to his memory.

We would not know so much about Hollis's character and motivation were it not for his extraordinary generosity to the Harvard College Library after its disastrous fire of 1764, and the high rate of survival of his many gifts over more than two centuries, which I judge to be close to 98 per cent. During the intervening years successive classification schemes dispersed Hollis books far and wide through a vast university library system, and despite diligent searching and the interested cooperation of many colleagues, I am certain that the two thousand or so titles that I have located by no means exhaust the inventory of his bounty, though they must represent a considerable preponderance of the total. They are surely more than sufficient to define his aims, and enough of them contain significant annotations to make his purpose and method abundantly clear. Reinforcing them at Harvard are the records and catalogues preserved in the University Archives, and two important resources acquired in modern times through the generosity of Mr Arthur A. Houghton, Jr: Hollis's unpublished holograph diary for the years 1758–70, and a large collection of drawings and proofs of engravings commissioned by Hollis from Giovanni Battista Cipriani and other artists, including Cipriani's original drawings for the emblematic tools.

Among the staff of the Harvard College Library I should single out for special thanks my friends Roger E. Stoddard, Rodney G. Dennis, Eleanor M. Garvey, Harley P. Holden, Richard J. Wolfe, Hugh Amory, James E. Walsh, Mollie Della Terza, Cynthia Naylor, Dennis Marnon, Joseph McCarthy, Peter Accardo, and the entire staff of the Houghton Reading Room, all of whom have at one time or another answered questions or ferreted out Hollis gifts that would otherwise have escaped my attention. Among other members of the Harvard community, Professors Mason Hammond and David Gordon Mitten have given indispensable assistance in dealing with Hollis's classical references and designs, as have Miss Agnes Mongan and Mrs Louise Ambler, of the staff of the Fogg Art Museum, on questions concerning the fine arts. Dr Cornelius Vermeule of the Boston Museum of Fine Arts was the first to suggest to me that several of Hollis's designs derive not from coins and medals but from friezes and intaglios.

The collegial gift to me of virtually the whole mass of Hollis materials accumulated by Professor Emerita Caroline Robbins of Bryn Mawr College has been of incalculable help, and I cannot adequately express my gratitude to her. Immensely helpful, too, have been the Hollisian notes passed down by earlier Harvard scholars such as Professors Chester Noyes Greenough and Henry J. Cadbury, and my friend and former colleague, G. W. Cottrell, Jr, first editor of the *Harvard Library Bulletin*. Other debts are acknowledged in text and footnotes.

My continued study of Hollis was greatly facilitated by the grant of a fellowship in 1982–83 by the John Simon Guggenheim Memorial Foundation, enabling me to extend my investigations far beyond the bounds of the Harvard College Library and thus enlarge the scope of the original Sandars Lectures. I wish in particular to record my gratitude to the Foundation's late President, Dr Gordon L. Ray.

Among many persons and institutions I wish especially to thank the Massachusetts Historical Society (Mr Peter Drummey, Dr Louis L. Tucker, Mr Conrad E. Wright); the Pierpont Morgan Library (Dr Anna Lou Ashby, former Director Charles Ryskamp, and Mr William Kmet); the Beinecke Rare Book and Manuscript Library at Yale (Miss Marjorie G. Wynne); the Princeton University Library (Mr Stephen Ferguson); the Humanities Research Center at the University of Texas, Austin (Dr John Chalmers); the British Library (Dr Mirjam M. Foot, who also contributed rubbings and notes on bindings in several other European libraries); the Royal Society of Arts (Mr D. G. C. Allan); Dr Williams's Library; the library of Christ's College, Cambridge (Dr and Mrs C. P. Courtney); the Stadt- und Universitätsbibliothek Bern (Mrs Margaret Eschler); the Zentralbibliothek Zürich (Herr Ludwig Kohler); and the Niedersächsische Staats- und Universitätsbibliothek, Göttingen (Dr Reimer Eck). Many of these extended far more than the usual courtesies by providing facilities for work, supplying photocopies, and answering many questions. I owe particular thanks to the Cambridge University Library for appointing me to the Readership and thus motivating me to bring to a focus hitherto occasional and diffuse work on Hollis; and especially to Dr Frederick W. Ratcliffe, University Librarian, and his colleagues Dr J. C. T. Oates, Mr R. P. Carr, Dr J. T. D. Hall, and Dr David McKitterick (now Librarian of Trinity College). During our stay in Cambridge, Mrs Bond and I enjoyed the generous and warm hospitality of Mrs A. N. L. Munby, who provided us with a welcome home away from home.

The Reverend Peter B. Godfrey, Minister of the Upper Chapel in

Sheffield, sent me invaluable information about the Hollis connection with the Chapel, the Hollis Hospital, and various other charities, and incidentally with clues I would not otherwise have discovered concerning Robert Thorner and his Trust. I am grateful to Mr Cyril Humphris of Cyril Humphris Ltd for the opportunity to study Joseph Wilton's monumental bust of Hollis, and for furnishing me with photographs and permitting me to reproduce them; likewise to Mr Patrick King of Patrick King Ltd, for a photograph and rubbings of a binding executed for Dr John Hawkesworth illustrated in his *Catalogue Thirteen*, also with permission to reproduce. I am indebted to Mr H. D. Lyon, Mr Howard S. Mott, Mr Robert H. Rubin, Mr W. R. Fletcher, Mr Arthur Freeman of Bernard Quaritch Ltd, and especially Mr George T. Goodspeed of Goodspeed's Book Shop for making available and in some cases presenting to me Hollis materials through the channels of the book trade. Indeed, the trade has always manifested a particular interest in Hollis bindings, and booksellers' catalogues contain many valuable illustrations.

Through the long years of my obsession with Thomas Hollis my family has shown exemplary patience, and for that I am profoundly grateful.

I

The anonymous republican

ON FRIDAY, 20 April 1781, Samuel Johnson and James Boswell spent what Boswell said was 'one of the happiest days that I remember to have enjoyed in the whole course of my life'. The occasion was a party given by the widow of David Garrick, her first social event since her husband's death in 1779. It was a small gathering of bluestockings and other literati, and limited to close friends of the Garricks. Boswell had such a good time that he confessed to being less than usually diligent and successful in recording the conversation, but he managed to reconstruct some of it, during the course of which an unexpected name cropped up. I quote the sketchier and less familiar version found in the rough notes of his journal. The curious may be interested to see for themselves how Boswell expanded, rearranged, and embroidered this raw material in his *Life of Johnson*.[1]

Before dinner Hollis was talked of. [Of course this is our eponymous hero, Thomas Hollis V, who had died in 1774.] Mrs Carter said he talked uncharitably of people. Dr. Johnson with great sophistry said, 'Who is the worse for being talked of uncharitably? Hollis was a dull, poor creature as ever lived.' He said he beleived [*sic*] Hollis would not have done harm to a Man of opposite principles. 'Once at the Society of Arts when an Advertisement was to be drawn up, he pointed me out as a Man who could do it best. This was kindness to me. I however slipt away.' Mrs. Carter doubted he was an Atheist. 'I don't know that,' said the Doctor, smiling. 'He might perhaps have become one if he had had time to ripen. He might have exuberated into an Atheist.'

And the conversation turned to other topics.

But one may wonder why it had turned to Thomas Hollis at all, that 'dull, poor creature', as they thought him, who had been dead nearly seven and a half years, and whose name appears nowhere else in Boswell's *Life*. The cause was probably the publication in 1780 of Archdeacon Francis Blackburne's monumental (and anonymous, and according to Horace Walpole, deadly dull) *Memoirs of Thomas Hollis*.

[1] *The Journal of James Boswell 1779–1781*, in *Private Papers of James Boswell* ed. Geoffrey Scott and Frederick A. Pottle (privately printed 1932) 14, p. 203; *Boswell's Life of Johnson* ed. G. B. Hill and L. F. Powell (Oxford 1934) 4, pp. 96–8.

I

In itself this hardly deserved the condescension of Dr Johnson and the spite of Mrs Carter. But in 1779, after the main text of the *Memoirs* had been set and printed, but before its publication, Johnson published the first volumes of his *Lives of the Poets*, in the second volume of which appeared his highly derogatory account of John Milton, a hero to both Blackburne and his deceased friend Hollis.

Blackburne wrote at white heat a spirited defence of Milton that was also a personal attack on Samuel Johnson. Fifty-four quarto pages were inserted in the middle of the *Memoirs of Thomas Hollis*; repeated and starred pagination and signatures make the insertion obvious,[1] and the text was also separately issued in a duodecimo edition uniform in size with Johnson's *Lives*. If the company at Mrs Garrick's table had not read Blackburne's attack, they must have known of it.

Blackburne freely acknowledged Johnson's literary stature and achievements, but strongly deplored his denigration of Milton as well as the turning of his pen against Whig republicanism and in favour of what Blackburne regarded as repression of civil and religious liberties. Of course it was neither the first nor the last manifestation of Johnson's deeply rooted High Church Toryism, opposite principles indeed to those held by Blackburne, who was the author of *The Confessional*, and by Hollis, the sturdy Dissenter who had laboured under the political and social disabilities of non-conformity in the eighteenth century.

Directly and in so many words Blackburne accused Johnson of literary prostitution. No wonder that 'Dr. Johnson *with great sophistry*' – we can now understand Boswell's choice of the word, which incidentally disappeared in the version to be found in the *Life* – no wonder Dr Johnson said, 'Who is the worse for being talked of uncharitably?' and lashed out at the subject of the *Memoirs*, their author being anonymous. Later you can judge these disparagements for yourselves; meantime, it may be noted that Johnson knew Hollis better and owed him more than he admitted, while Boswell thought enough of Hollis to present to him a specially bound copy of his *Account of Corsica*.[2]

Because there is a profusion – Dr Johnson might have said an exuberance – of Thomas Hollises, let me identify the one who is my

[1] Pp. *533–84* (rectos and versos are alternately preceded and followed by the asterisk).
[2] W. H. Bond 'Thomas Hollis and Samuel Johnson' in *Johnson and His Age* ed. James Engell (Cambridge, Mass. 1984), pp. 83–105. On Boswell's gift to Hollis, see *The Rothschild Catalogue* (Cambridge 1954) I, p. 89 no. 447. Clearly Boswell knew Hollis better than he chose to reveal either in the *Life* or in his journals.

subject, and explain how he became so deeply involved with Harvard College. Thomas Hollis of Lincoln's Inn was the fifth and last of that name, the descendant and heir of a tribe of wealthy and successful manufacturers and merchants, Dissenters in religion and Old Whigs in politics. The first Thomas Hollis prospered as a whitesmith and cutler in Rotherham in the West Riding of Yorkshire, where he died in 1663. He founded the Sheffield Hospital, a charity to maintain sixteen poor cutlers' widows, and was a mainstay of the Upper Chapel in Sheffield; both institutions exist to this day. His eldest son, the second Thomas, the only child of his first wife Ellen (Ramskar), was born in Rotherham in 1634, and was apprenticed at the age of fourteen to his uncle, John Ramskar, also a cutler. In 1654 Ramskar sent Thomas II to his London office, where he eventually set up as an independent merchant. He died there in 1718. He and his wife, Anne (Thorner), worshipped at Pinner's Hall, London's leading Independent Meeting House, and in 1679 he secured a ninety-nine-year lease of the Hall, which was served during most of the eighteenth century by a line of distinguished Dissenting ministers including Isaac Watts and Caleb Fleming, all closely associated with the Hollis family.

It was through Thomas II and his brother-in-law Robert Thorner that the Hollis family first became involved with the fortunes of Harvard College. Early in 1688 the Reverend Increase Mather of Boston in the Massachusetts Bay Colony travelled to London, partly to escape legal persecution at the hands of Edward Randolph, but even more to try to negotiate the terms of a new charter for the colony to replace the old royal charter, which had been declared forfeit in 1684. The colonists wished to avoid provisions disadvantageous to Dissenters and to have more control over their legislative affairs.

The cancellation of the charter of the colony clearly threatened to invalidate Harvard College's charter of 1650 which depended on it, and to eliminate at a stroke the President and Fellows, and the Board of Overseers, the College's two governing bodies. Its governance was already in a precarious state. After the death of President John Rogers in 1684 no one could be found who was both qualified and willing to fill the vacancy. Increase Mather was induced to become *Praeses pro tempore* while continuing to devote most of his time and energy to his duties as minister of the Second Church in Boston. In 1686 Joseph Dudley received the royal commission as President of the Council for New England, and replaced the elected General Court with an appointed Council. Harvard's governing boards were indeed eliminated. To take

3

their place, Dudley named Mather to be Rector of the College and entrusted its management to him and to Tutors John Leverett and William Brattle. But the College was not safe, for there were those in England and America who viewed it with suspicion and hostility. The securing of a new College charter seemed essential for its preservation.

Mather's embassy, which included the closing days of the reign of James II and the beginning of that of William and Mary, lasted until 1692 and ended with a qualified success. The Colonial charter that eventually emerged was not all that the colonists might have desired. Most colonial administrators were still appointed by the Crown without much (or indeed any) participation by those administered, but the elective legislature was restored; and there was nothing that directly threatened Harvard College. In the end, after no fewer than eight revisions of its constitution, in 1708 Harvard reverted to the form prescribed by the Charter of 1650.[1]

Mather took advantage of his London sojourn to gain a wide acquaintance in court and government circles, and even more so in the ranks of the leading Dissenters. Among these were Thomas II and his brother-in-law, Robert Thorner, both of whom became interested in Harvard, and thus began the family's long relationship with the college. Thorner's will, executed in 1690, included a provision for £500 to be given to Harvard upon the expiration of certain long leases; because of this peculiarity it was known as 'Thorner's Trust', and was not wound up until 1775. Thomas II and III, among others, served as Thorner's executors, and successive members of the Hollis family became trustees of the complicated legacy, until eventually Thomas V and his cousin Timothy bore the sometimes vexing responsibility. Over the many years of its life there were sundry lawsuits concerning boundaries and rights of way, and other beneficiaries than Harvard were involved.[2]

With all this, the second Thomas did not forget his Midland origins,

---

[1] Much more detail about Increase Mather in England may be found in Kenneth Ballard Murdock *Increase Mather, the Foremost American Puritan* (Cambridge, Mass. 1925), pp. 155–286; on Hollis, Thorner, and Harvard, see pp. 276–8. For the tangled affairs of the College at this period, see Samuel Eliot Morison *Harvard in the Seventeenth Century* (Cambridge, Mass. 1936), pp. 472–88.

[2] Thus Timothy wrote to Thomas, 16 April 1772. 'What Ridiculous foolish Things these Trusts are founded in Vanity Superstition & a false Notion of Goodness You know My Sentiments of them these Many Years Past Were it not for their being so Connected with My family & Ancestors I wᵈ. have Nothing to do with them But being thus Unavoidably Engaged I think My self Obliged to do My Best while I am Able. . .' (from Timothy's retained copy in Harvard, MS Eng 1191.1).

for he helped to found the Dissenters' meeting-hall in Sheffield, the Upper Chapel; endowed a Free School there for tradesmen's and artificers' children; and augmented the foundation of the Sheffield Hospital. The latter two charities also came to be a worrisome charge for Thomas V and his cousin Timothy, for both the Hollis School and the Hospital suffered dilapidations and other unanticipated problems.[1]

Thomas II's eldest son was the third Thomas Hollis, who twice married but died without issue in 1730. As one of the trustees of Thorner's Trust, he was kept in touch with the affairs of Harvard College. He was the first of the Hollis name to be a major benefactor. Others of his generation and the next also helped the small college in the other Cambridge, but curiously enough none of the seventeenth- or eighteenth-century Hollises ever crossed the Atlantic to inspect the college for themselves. Their good works were founded on faith, reinforced by the reports of travellers, correspondents, and agents in and from the New World.

It was Thomas Hollis III who established the Hollis Professorships in Divinity and in Natural Philosophy, the oldest chairs at Harvard, indeed in North America; and he provided other benefits as well, amounting in all to at least £5,000, a very large sum for those days. If Harvard's money managers had followed today's practices, his and later Hollis endowments would be among its largest. But until relatively recent times they were carried on the books at their original amount, and they remain relatively modest. The Hollis gifts were so useful that the President and Fellows named one of the new buildings in the College for the donor. (Thorner's Trust, however, survives only as a few sentences in histories of the College. Its proceeds were not set up as a separate endowment, but simply absorbed into the general funds.)

With his brothers Nathaniel and John, the third Thomas was also generous to charities in England, re-founding the Sheffield Hospital (later known as Hollis Hospital) and supporting Baptist and Independent religious societies. The fourth Thomas Hollis was the eldest son of

---

[1] For information about the Upper Chapel in Sheffield, the Sheffield Hospital Trust, and Thorner's Trust I am indebted to the Reverend Peter B. Godfrey, BA, present Minister of the Upper Chapel, who kindly answered questions and sent photocopies of newspaper cuttings and an excellent article by Malcolm Mercer 'The Hollis Educational Trust: A Nonconformist Contribution to Elementary Education' *Transactions of the Hunter Archaeological Society* (1938), pp. 68 ff. The Chapel, now located in Norfolk Street, is Unitarian though originally designated as Presbyterian. The Hospital continues with its original purpose as Hollis's Hospital, but is now governed by the local authority rather than its traditional Board of Trustees.

Nathaniel, and the fifth Thomas Hollis – our subject – was the son of Thomas IV.

Thomas Hollis V was born in London on 14 April 1720 – an anniversary he never failed to observe with pious meditations and honourable resolutions, faithfully recorded in his *Diary*. Mrs Carter, among others, 'doubted he was an Atheist'. On the contrary, he was deeply religious, but simply no church-goer. Even the most independent Dissenting sect sooner or later established regulations, often as strict as those of the Church of England or the Church of Rome. Hollis reacted strongly against all man-made ecclesiastical forms and rules, and could find no congregation in which he felt wholly comfortable.

Meanwhile he exhibited Lockeian toleration for those whose views did not agree with his own. Thus, in his twenties, when the acquisition of estates in Dorset brought him the bestowal of several livings in the Church of England, the strictest Anglican could not have been more punctilious in making sure that the church authorities approved his choices, and that the duties of the parish would be faithfully discharged by the incumbent. Indeed, Hollis had a wide and close acquaintance with churchmen of every stripe, from the Archbishop of Canterbury to such latitudinarians as his own biographer, Blackburne. His friends and correspondents included Roman Catholics, Jews, Quakers, and Dissenters of every sect; all he required was that no man should attempt to regulate the views or restrict the liberties of any other.

Most of what we know of his early life comes from the *Memoirs*. His earliest years were spent with his maternal grandparents, Mr and Mrs Scott of Wolverhampton. He began formal education not many miles away at the Free School in Newport, and after four or five years he was put under a tutor at St Albans. A writing-master, one Mr Fuller, taught him the handsome, vigorous, and legible hand that he employed to the end of his life. At the age of thirteen he was sent to Amsterdam, to learn accounting and the Dutch and French languages, and generally to prepare to return to London and take his part in the family business.

But when Thomas was only fifteen, his father died, leaving him sole heir, destined to become at his majority a wealthy man. John Hollister, then Treasurer of Guy's Hospital (of which Thomas was later a Trustee), became his guardian. A career in public service seemed to open before him, and a liberal education was now to be added to the practical training he had already acquired.

But what kind of a liberal education? He began a private course of study, partly because the only way to the two Universities for a

Dissenter was through the hypocrisy of occasional conformity, and partly because the Universities did not really offer the curriculum he desired. This was to be modelled with evident intention on that prescribed nearly a century earlier in John Milton's letter to Samuel Hartlib, *Of Education*. The similarity between his career and that laid down by Milton is too close to be dismissed as mere coincidence; the only difference was that Hollis's circumstances caused him to begin somewhat later in life. His formal studies as well as his subsequent activities were directed with extraordinary fidelity to Milton's plan, which Hollis always referred to as a 'MASTER tract', while he lost no opportunity to point out that Milton had 'exhausted' the subject 'in one single sheet'. Bibliographers will recall that the first edition does indeed occupy the eight pages of one quarto sheet. Hollis knew it well, and it was in his personal library.[1] He heartily approved the aim of such an education: to fit 'a man to perform justly, skilfully, and magnanimously all the offices, both private and public, of peace and war'. 'Magnanimity' became another of Hollis's watchwords.

In addition to the scholastic pursuits advocated by Milton, Hollis engaged all his life in fencing and riding for exercise, and followed the injunction that one's diet should be 'plain, healthful, and moderate'. Apart from those few pupils Milton himself had taught, one may doubt that anyone else ever followed the syllabus so faithfully.

His tutor was Dr John Ward (1679?–1758), Professor of Rhetoric at Gresham College, a learned man and distinguished teacher. Young Hollis received a thorough grounding in Latin and Greek and a familiarity with the classics as well as with natural science, together with a considerable proficiency in Italian – all in accordance with Milton's doctrine. He also developed a love of classical antiquities and a taste and eye for the fine arts that he cultivated for the rest of his life. Later, when on the Grand Tour, he wrote to his old teacher detailed accounts of the latest archaeological discoveries at Pompeii and Herculaneum, and sent him James Stuart's handwritten prospectus for the proposed visit to Greece that eventually resulted in the famous *Antiquities of Athens* (1762).[2]

In Thomas's eighteenth year his grandfather Nathaniel died, adding another considerable fortune to that already in trust. More than most

---

[1] In a set of four tract volumes, lot 934 in the Hollis–Disney sale, Sotheby, 1817.

[2] Letters written from Italy and elsewhere to John Ward are found in B.L. Add. MS. 6210, ff. 130, 139, 141, 143, 147–9, and Add. MS. 4443, f. 138. The prospectus for Stuart and Revett's *Antiquities* is in Add. MS. 6210, f. 135.

young middle-class men of his day he could afford to enlarge his experience of the world, explore its possibilities, and follow without stint his chosen direction. His family background of strong Whigs and staunch Dissenters had formed in him powerful convictions about social responsibility and the importance of defending civil and religious freedom. The rest of his life testifies to his seriousness of purpose. Although he was generous with his ample means, his early commercial training made him a good manager; even his cousin Timothy Hollis, some years older and a man of business all his days, turned to Thomas for financial advice.

Again in accordance with Milton's precepts, his first venture into the larger world was to study the law by gaining admission to Lincoln's Inn, where in February 1740 he took up residence at No. 6, New Square.[1] Always thereafter he proudly denominated himself 'Thomas Hollis of Lincoln's Inn', but we do not know how seriously he contemplated a legal career, and he was never called to the Bar. Little documentation survives for his studies there. A volume that he later gave to Harvard had once belonged to one William Bohun of Lincoln's Inn, and in it Hollis noted that Bohun was a 'strenuous Advocate for civil & religious Liberty', adding that in 1742 he attended Bohun's private lectures on English law.[2] An extra mark of Hollis's respect was to inscribe in the book a favourite quotation from Petrarch, 'Che trae l'uom del Sepolcro, ed in vita il serba.'[3]

According to Miltonic doctrine, such studies were intended to prepare for public service. Without doubt Hollis was thereafter both attracted and repelled by the possibility of a career in the House of Commons – attracted because of the good he might do, and repelled because the distasteful path to election required the empty form of

---

[1] A chronology of Hollis's lodgings in London and Dorset may be helpful: 1735–February 1740, while studying with Dr John Ward, probably in the London home of his guardian, John Hollister; February 1740–19 July 1748, No. 6, New Square, Lincoln's Inn; then until some time in 1753, possibly April, touring the continent; 1753–23 January 1761, rooms in the house of Mrs Mott, Bedford Sreet, Covent Garden (terminated by a fire); briefly at the Old Hummums, Covent Garden (a combination Turkish bath, coffee house, and hotel) while searching for new quarters; 1 February 1761–July 1770, Piccadilly at the corner of John Street, a house leased from Mrs Leighton, and maintained as a *pied-à-terre* until his death, 1 January 1774. In Dorset he had no fixed residence, but stayed in the farmhouse, Urles Farm, parish of Corscombe, or in a suite of rooms in the Three Cups, Lyme Regis, as suited his convenience; meantime he continued to search for a permanent residence in the general neighbourhood. His *Diary* contains much evidence that he was hard to suit.

[2] The book is *Oratio Dominica* ed. John Chamberlayne (Amsterdam 1715); Harvard, *EC7.C3555.7150.   [3] *Trionfi* 1.

8

occasional conformity and most often led through rotten boroughs and bought electors. In later life he was several times offered safe seats. He always declined, as he also declined office in some of the learned and charitable societies to which he belonged, preferring to enact his chosen rôle as a private citizen without danger of compromising his principles. As he once wrote to one of his American friends, Edmund Quincy III, he lived the life of 'a sober, retired Person, without a by-view'.

Ironically enough, less than a year after Hollis died, his close friend and heir Thomas Brand (who, when he inherited, took the name Brand Hollis) was persuaded to stand for the small Wiltshire borough of Hindon, was betrayed by a political manager who gave unauthorized bribes, and was crucified by the Tory majority, most of whom had won their seats by exactly the same methods.[1] The manager escaped scot-free, but Brand Hollis was deprived of his seat, sent to King's Bench Prison for six months, and fined 1,000 marks, somewhat more than £650 – a brutal lesson for a naïve Dissenting Whig, and one that Thomas Hollis's own resolution enabled him to avoid. But it was principle, not fear, that governed Thomas Hollis's actions.

Hollis maintained residence in New Square for nearly ten years, and whatever his legal studies, he appears to have engaged in good works rather than the many dissolute activities open to young men of means in London. Among his benefactions was a generous subscription for the relief of veterans of the force sent against the uprising of 1745 in Scotland. The '45 seems to have made a great impression on him. He equipped himself with a pair of silver-mounted pistols in case the insurrection swept on to London; but more important than that, it probably planted the seeds of his one fixed and immovable illiberal belief, shared with Brand Hollis and with numerous of his friends among the Dissenting clergy: prejudice against the Roman Catholic Church, which he considered to be not so much a church as a government meddling with other governments. How strong his prejudice was may be seen from his inscription in the Harvard copy of Samuel Morland *The History of the Evangelical Churches of the Valleys of Piemont* (London 1658),[2]

---

[1] [John Disney] *Memoirs of Thomas Brand-Hollis* (London 1808), pp. 10–12.

[2] c 7866.58*. The massacre of the Waldensians took place on 24 April 1655. Hollis must also have known Milton's sonnet 'On the Late Massacre in Piemont'. Sir Samuel Morland carried Cromwell's formal protest (written by Milton) to the Duke of Savoy and brought back documentation of the atrocities, which he gave to the Cambridge University Library in 1658; see J. C. T. Oates *Cambridge University Library, a History from the Beginnings to the Copyright Act of Queen Anne* (Cambridge [1986]), pp. 283–8.

a book adorned with graphic cuts of the martyrdom of Protestants at the hands of Roman Catholic troops:

> Reader, Whomsoever thou mayest be that shalt peruse these lines, whether Pagan or Jew, Christian or Mohammedan or Sceptic, consider well the Doctrines, Practices, Massacres of the Papists; and, so long as the arm of Popery is uplifted against thee, so long be thine uplifted against Popery, in justice to thyself and to Mankind.

Of course his feelings were aggravated by the disabilities under which Dissenters laboured in England, which seemed less likely to be alleviated by governmental action than those of Catholics. But his anti-Catholic bias did not extend to individuals. He never forgot the kindness and hospitality he experienced in certain Roman Catholic establishments, notably the monastery at Catania in Sicily, and he liked, admired, and materially assisted many Catholic friends both in England and on the continent.

As soon as he reached his majority he began to acquire extensive farmland in Dorset. In this he was again following Milton's advice to engage in the practical study of agricultural science. Although most of his early and middle years were spent in London or abroad, he evidently took a direct part in the management of his farms. When his favourite old saddle-horse Hob, long retired from active service, had to be destroyed in 1766, Hollis noted that he had bred the animal at Urles Farm in the spring of 1748.[1] But until he retired from London in 1770, he had to leave the day-to-day supervision of his country properties and their farmers to a trusted steward, Peter Maber.

By the time of his death in 1774, Hollis owned about 3,000 acres in Dorset. Most of the land was bought from the distressed Earl of Pomfret (who had fled to France to escape the bailiffs) and lay in the parishes of Corscombe and Halstock, from fifteen to twenty miles from Lyme Regis, a town greatly admired by Hollis.[2] Towards the end of his life he tried unsuccessfully to find not only a suitable house for himself in Lyme but also one for the elder Pitt, a life-long sufferer from gout and other chronic ailments; Hollis thought the town unequalled for beauty of location and salubrious air. It may be why he chose to build an estate in Dorset, though the Hollis family must have been familiar with the county because Robert Thorner, brother-in-law of Thomas II and

---

[1] *Diary* 4 July 1766.
[2] B. L. Add. MS. 34733, f. 150, contains a letter from Hollis to James West concerning negotiations for the purchase, consummated in 1741. West (1704?–72) was a barrister then residing in Lincoln's Inn. He was a notable antiquarian and book collector, FRS, FSA, and a member of the Spalding Gentlemen's Society.

creator of the Thorner Trust, appears to have had holdings there.

As for the political situation of Lyme, that was quite different. Its government and its Parliamentary representation were tightly controlled by John Fane, 7th Earl of Westmorland, a notorious absentee who did not even own much property there, and who acted in all matters without regard for the local inhabitants. Such a state of affairs, so obvious to anyone on the scene, may have had much to do with settling Hollis's opinions concerning Parliamentary corruption. Of course he himself was an absentee landlord for all but the last few years of his life, but he kept in close touch with his lands and tenants through Maber, and with occasional visits of inspection he managed his Dorset farms responsibly and well. While some neighbouring tycoons in the West Country changed the landscape, moved or rebuilt whole villages, and raised pompous mansions and elaborate gardens, Hollis preserved and improved the farms he had bought, which had fallen into disrepair in Pomfret's hands, and encouraged his tenants to work them in traditional ways.

In July of 1748 Hollis stored his most prized books and other possessions in his cousin Timothy's City of London house in St Mary Axe, and prepared to follow Milton's last piece of educational advice by going on the Grand Tour. Milton's tract recommends foreign travel as the culmination of a proper education. After following the curriculum to that point, young hopefuls would have no need of foreign cicerones who might lead them into foolish airs and graces; instead,

if they desire to see other countries at three or four and twenty years of age, not to learn principles, but to enlarge experience, and make wise observations, they will by that time be such as shall deserve the regard and honour of all men where they pass, and the society and friendship of those in all places who are best and most eminent.

Hollis was a few years late in following this advice, for he had begun late, and perhaps he had also been deterred by the posture of international affairs.

Whatever the reason, on 19 July 1748 he set out with his friend Thomas Brand on the first of two long tours of the continent that together lasted almost six years and extended through Europe from Scandinavia to Italy, where he spent most of his time. Hollis and Brand took separate paths on their second tour, though they joined forces now and again.

Hollis was probably well supplied with introductions, and as he proceeded he was recommended to yet other eminent and interesting persons. He certainly prepared himself by listing those he most wished to meet. For example, a three-volume anonymous guidebook, *Roma Antica e Moderna* (1750),[1] which he transferred to Harvard in 1768, bears in his hand on a flyleaf of volume I thirty-three names of persons, both Italians and English expatriates, ranging from scholars and antiquaries through painters and engravers to picture-framers and one 'Maestro Alichini in the Piazza di Spagna' who 'makes Tables & paintings to immitate [*sic*] the antient Mosaic Work'. Among this company are Piranesi; the Abbate Venuti, whose work on the Roman liberty-cap was later written at the request of Hollis, who in 1762 imported fifty copies in sheets to be bound for distribution;[2] Domenicho Landi, antiquary to Cardinal Albani, one of the most notable Roman collectors; and the English painters Richard Wilson and Thomas Jenkins, who in 1752 and 1753 painted portraits of Hollis and Brand, respectively.[3]

Others among his European acquaintance, both native and transplanted Englishmen, turn up later in his diary as correspondents and authors of books acquired by purchase or gift: a surprising number of Sicilian intellectuals and antiquaries, including Gabriele Lancilotto Castello, Prince of Torremuzza, and two successive priors of the Benedictine monastery at Catania, which had been hospitable to the traveller; that curious and ambiguous figure in the courts of Europe, Count Francesco Algarotti, popularizer of Newton for ladies, who at one time was ardently pursued by Lord Hervey and Lady Mary Wortley Montagu, and at another by Frederick II of Prussia;[4] British consuls the length of Italy, including Tatem at Messina, Allen at

---

[1] Typ 725.50.750 (B).

[2] Ridolfino Venuti *De dea libertate ejusque cultu apud Romanos et De libertinorum pileo Dissertatio* . . . (Rome 1762). See *Diary* 15 August 1762.

[3] Wilson's portrait of Hollis hangs in the office of the Librarian of Harvard College, the gift of Mr and Mrs Donald F. Hyde. It was sold as part of the estate of Edgar Norton Disney, Sotheby, 8 March 1950, lot 134. According to W. G. Constable *Richard Wilson* (Cambridge, Mass. [1953]), p. 32, it is 'the only portrait proper [Wilson] is known to have painted in Rome'. That of Brand by Jenkins was sold at Sotheby–Parke Bernet, New York, 16 June 1977, lot 220A (illustration in catalogue), present location unknown. On Jenkins's activities in Rome, see John Fleming 'Some Roman Cicerones and Artist–Dealers' *The Connoisseur Year Book* (London 1959), pp. 24–7.

[4] Hollis's influence on Algarotti appears on the engraved frontispiece and title-page of his *Opere* (Leghorn 1764), which (along with Masonic symbols, the three Graces, and a double row of sculptured heads on square classical pillars) display Hollis's owl, lyre, and palm and olive branches. Algarotti's tomb also includes several of Hollis's emblems. See also George Truett Hollis 'Count Francesco Algarotti and the Society for the Encouragement of Arts, Manufactures and Commerce' *Journal of the Royal Society of Arts* 123 (1975), pp. 605–7, 668–71, 728–30. By a curious coincidence, Algarotti's *Il Neutonianismo per le dame* was translated into English by Mrs Elizabeth Carter and proofread by Dr Johnson in 1739.

1   Oil portrait of Thomas Hollis by Richard Wilson, 1752

Naples, the celebrated Joseph Smith at Venice, and Dodsworth on the island of Malta; booksellers, wherever he went; and many artists, possibly including Canaletto, from whom he later commissioned six paintings during the artist's visit to England;[1] and the aforementioned Piranesi, to whom in 1769 he sent a handsome shagreen case of drawing instruments made by none other than the celebrated Benjamin Martin of London.[2]

We cannot say when be began to apply himself seriously to collecting books, classical antiquities, coins, medals, and works of art, but I suspect the acquisitive instinct and discrimination so evident later were already well developed, and that he began his habitual frequenting of shops and sale-rooms before he even left Lincoln's Inn. 'Bought during my Travels in Paris [or Naples, or Rome, or Florence, or the like]' appears often enough in good books eventually given to Harvard to afford strong evidence that he was no newcomer to collecting before he returned to London, or even before he left it in the first place. He was fascinated by the archaeological discoveries constantly being made at Pompeii, Herculaneum, and Paestum, as he had been with James Stuart's plans for recording the antiquities at Athens, and he evidently communicated them as soon as he could to his learned friends in London. And with all this intellectual activity he continued his Miltonian régime of exercise by taking fencing lessons when he found opportunity.[3]

---

[1] W. G. Constable *Canaletto* (Oxford 1962) I, pp. 21, 40–2, 145; II, no. 396, 'The Piazza del Campidoglio', pp. 368–9; no. 420, 'Ranelagh, interior of the Rotunda', pp. 383–4; no. 422, 'St Paul's Cathedral', p. 384; no. 437b, 'Westminster Bridge', pp. 394–5; no. 441, 'Old Walton Bridge', p. 397; no. 472, 'Capriccio: buildings in Whitehall', p. 412. No. 420 is in the National Gallery, no. 441 in Dulwich Gallery, London. Nos. 396 and 441 both include a group of three figures in the foreground, evidently intended to represent Hollis, Brand, and Hollis's Italian servant, Francesco Giovannini; clothing and posture are similar though not identical in the two paintings, and the dominant figure is apparently Hollis. No. 396 was sold at Christie's (London) in 1973; no. 472 at Christie's (New York) in 1984. See also notes by Francis Haskell and others in *Canaletto* ed. Alessandro Bettagno ([Venice 1952]), pp. 77–9; Joseph G. Links *Canaletto and His Patrons* (New York 1977), pp. 76–8. Links mistakenly attributes to Hollis's collection 'Greenwich Hospital' (Constable no. 414, now in the National Maritime Museum, Greenwich) and 'Eton College Chapel' (Constable no. 450, now in the National Gallery, London), neither of which has a Hollis provenance.   [2] *Memoirs*, pp. 421, 712.

[3] Hollis gave the Harvard Library a battered textbook on fencing inscribed to him in 1752 in Naples by his teachers, the brothers Saverio and Domenico Bosco (H 5695.50*). Milton also recommended wrestling as an exercise; Hollis sent to Harvard a copy of Nicolaes Petter *Klare Onderrichtinge der voortreffelijke Worstel-konst* (Amsterdam 1674), a handbook on the subject with engraved illustrations by Romeyn de Hooghe (Typ 632.74.683) inscribed, 'Manly Exercises cannot be too much encouraged by ingenuous, that is free, Nations.'

Hollis's personal contacts were obviously illuminating and satisfactory, though we would like to know more about them. When Blackburne compiled the *Memoirs* he had before him seven holograph journals of those six years abroad, as well as a small notebook of expenses. They survived at least until 1808, when the Reverend John Disney mentioned them in his memoir of Brand Hollis, but they have since disappeared and may have been destroyed during the closing of a country house, or through some other accident. Although Blackburne devoted more than fifty pages to excerpts, he chose mainly descriptive or impressionistic passages about landscapes and buildings, and revealed little of Hollis's opinions beyond the usual observations of a traveller. Blackburne also listed some of the persons Hollis met, but little or nothing of their interactions and conversations. Disney's memoir of Brand Hollis is even less informative. There must also have been a quantity of correspondence with many people, especially since Hollis habitually retained copies of significant letters. How extensive that correspondence was, and what an important part it played in Hollis's career, may be seen in the note proposing him for membership in the Royal Society, which cites his interest in 'polite literature' and his zeal in promoting 'all useful knowledge' (standard attributes of most candidates), and then goes on exceptionally to say, 'by his foreign correspondence [he is] capable of becoming a very worthy and valuable member'. In the event, a number of distinguished foreign members were elected to that and other learned societies through nomination by Hollis.[1]

Other useful evidence still exists. In September 1760, Hollis wrote a long memorandum for a young man, William Taylor Howe,[2] who was about to visit Italy for the first time. All but the first four pages survive, packed with specific advice about persons and places, closing with such practical maxims as,

No Virtu, of any kind, to be purchased in Italy for the first six months; and with great caution afterwards. Modern books, & old books of places, only to be bought in Italy. Books of old editions to be met with much cheaper elsewhere. In England especially... Accidents almost always unfavorable to a Traveller, and augment his

---

[1] For the nominations of Brand and Hollis to the Royal Society, see B.L. Add. MS. 6180, ff. 247–247^v. Both before and after his election (on 17 March 1757), Hollis suggested appropriate foreign members; for a few examples, see Add. MS. 6210, ff. 145, 148^v, 149; Add. MS. 4443, ff. 138–9, 151, 180.

[2] B.L. Add. MS. 26899; *Diary* 10, 12, 14, 18, 24, and 27 September 1760. For photocopies of the Howe letters (later checked against the originals in the British Library), and for many other kindnesses, I am deeply indebted to Professor Caroline Robbins.

Expences a fifth. . . English Company, English Customs, English Dress, English Houses, English Retainers, FOR THE GENERAL to be avoided in Italy. Information, Advice by no means to be relied on unless the Views, Connections, Character of the Person are fully considered & known.

This is the voice of experience (which Hollis reinforced by the gift of the pistols he had bought for himself in 1745), all the more noteworthy because Hollis must have been among the earliest scions of the rising middle class to take the Grand Tour. And the general impressions he received were crucial in defining his philosophy and the plan of action to which he devoted the rest of his life.

There is an interesting parallel in Professor J. W. Burrow's study of nineteenth-century Whig historians, *A Liberal Descent*, ascribing at least some of the Victorian liberal and anti-Catholic bias to the experience of travellers on the Grand Tour. Burrow writes,

The more progressive tendencies of Protestant communities spoke eloquently for the reformed religion, supplementing more purely theological considerations. The increasing diffusion and scope of continental travel provided material for an informal sociology of religion; the state of inns and beds brought opportunities for inductive Protestant apologetics, and pyrrhic victories for the purer faith. Catholicism was clearly associated with poverty, flies, dirt and indolence, as well as priestcraft and intolerance.[1]

It was not a Victorian phenomenon. A century before the travellers of whom Professor Burrow writes, we find Hollis summarizing his own continental experience thus, in a birthday effusion dated 14 April 1753, the year when he returned to England:

I have seen the specious vain Frenchman, the trucking scrub Dutchman; the tame, lost Dane; the sturdy, self-righting Swede; the barbarous Russ; the turbulent Pole; the honest, dull German; the pay-fighting Swiss; the subtile, splendid Italian; the salacious Turk; the ever warring, lounging Maltese; the piratical Moor; the proud, cruel Spaniard; the bigotted, base Portugal; their countries; and hail again, Old England, my native land!

Reader, (if Englishman, Scotchman, Irishman) rejoice in the freedom, that is, the felicity of thine own country: and maintain it sacred to posterity!

This he wrote in a manuscript, now lost but seen and recorded by Blackburne, who says that Hollis also scratched it on the window of an inn at Falmouth:[2] could that have been the port of entry on his return from the continent?

At first glance, one scarcely knows how seriously to take this almost

---

[1] *A Liberal Descent: Victorian Historians and the English Past* (Cambridge and New York 1981), pp. 244–5.　　[2] *Memoirs*, p. 484.

comical outburst of chauvinism, but I need hardly say that mutual distrust on either side of the Channel was not new then and is not lacking now. Hollis had been prepared for this feeling by hints in Milton as well as the writings of one of his Whig heroes of the early eighteenth century, Lord Molesworth, who had declared in print that one of the chief benefits of foreign travel was to show at first hand the advantages of British liberty as contrasted with varying degrees of foreign despotism and misrule. Not everyone thought, as did Laurence Sterne, one of Hollis's later acquaintances, that in France 'they order these things better'.

The birthday meditation, or polemic in this case, was echoed in part by a quotation from Thucydides that Hollis later wrote in many of the books to which he felt it applied: 'Felicity is Freedom, & Freedom is Magnanimity!'[1] He found another congenial sentiment in Mark Akenside's *Odes*, Book I, viii, written in 1744 when Hollis and Akenside's good friend Jeremiah Dyson were both resident in Lincoln's Inn. This poem, 'On Leaving Holland', makes much the same point. Its closing stanzas hail Freedom as 'great Citizen of Albion', and continue:

> . . . Thee
> Heroic Valour still attends,
> And useful Science, pleased to see
> How Art her studious toil extends:
> While Truth, diffusing from on high
> A lustre unconfined as day,
> Fills and commands the public eye:
> Till, pierced and sinking by her powerful ray,
> Tame Faith and monkish Awe, like nightly demons, fly.
>
> Hence the whole land the patriot's ardour shares:
> Hence dread Religion dwells with social Joy;
> And holy passions and unsullied cares,
> In youth, in age, domestic life employ.
> O fair Britannia, hail! With partial love,
> The tribes of men their native seats approve,
> Unjust and hostile to a foreign fame:
> But when from generous minds and manly laws
> A nation holds her prime applause,
> There public zeal defies the test of blame.[2]

[1] Identified by Professor Mason Hammond as an idiosyncratic paraphrase of Thucydides II.43.4, from the oration ascribed to Pericles.

[2] Hollis preferred to quote the first edition of 1745; Akenside made considerable revisions in the second edition of 1760. Hollis was familiar with both.

Hollis copied the final stanza on the flyleaves of many of the books he prepared for distribution to institutions and individuals. Most often he simply quoted 'O fair Britannia, hail!' He used that quotation as the caption of one of the most carefully planned of the patriotic etchings he commissioned from his Italian protégé, Giovanni Battista Cipriani. It was prominent on several of the commemorative medals that he jointly designed with James Stuart. Hollis also had it tooled in gold on some of his most elaborate bookbindings, including his own copy of Molesworth. As we shall see, his acquaintance Jonas Hanway borrowed the phrase for some of his own emblematic bindings. When Hollis was asked to subscribe to the re-casting of a number of bells for country churches, he made his subscription depend upon having the words cast on the bells themselves. Such a bell is said still to exist in the parish church at Corscombe in Dorset, and others may also survive. In January 1769 he prescribed the same motto for a bell to be cast for a church in Lyme Regis.

All this is not quite the digression it might seem. Hollis's Grand Tours reinforced the precepts inculcated by his Miltonic education; his observation of the domestic scene, and the political disabilities under which he suffered as a Dissenter, persuaded him that he could act most effectively if he did so as a private citizen. His financial means freed him to proceed as he thought best. As he confided to his friend, the Reverend Andrew Eliot of Boston, Massachusetts, in a letter of 25 May 1769,

Many years ago, upon the return from my Travells, six years Travel, I resolved, that the flower of my Life & Judgment, should be devoted, solely, as I was able, to the Service of my Country and Whole-Mankind. That Resolution has been carried into execution with *rigid energy* and an exceeding of three Years above my Plan; and, I thank God, by his Bounty, all things, & more, have been executed, have succeeded, that could be proposed from it.[1]

There are many other references to his 'Plan' in correspondence and in his *Diary*, but none more detailed than that; and all those that hint at its duration agree in suggesting that he originally intended to carry it out in ten years, and that he began it in 1754, shortly after his return to England.

The absence of a full-blown definition of the Plan leads one to suspect that it set forth goals rather than details of the means of attaining them. The means are to be deduced from Hollis's activities, which changed

---

[1] Original in the Hollis Papers, Massachusetts Historical Society; quoted by permission of Dr Louis L. Tucker, Director.

with changing circumstances. Through them all the theme of patriotism runs clear and strong. The ebb and flow of England's fortunes in the Seven Years' War; the bungling (as he viewed it) of the Peace of Paris; the opportunities that he saw for the advancement of knowledge and commerce through sundry learned societies; the hope of a new political beginning in the accession of the young George III, soon to be dimmed by what Hollis regarded as the malign influence of Bute; the flagrant abuse of the franchise evident in the Wilkes affair and similar political skirmishes; the enfranchisement of Roman Catholics in the colonial legislature of Grenada and the establishment of a Catholic bishop in Canada; and above all, what Hollis perceived as the growing mismanagement of the North American colonies – these and other events caused him to shift tactics as he deemed appropriate, and to extend the Plan a full five years beyond his original intention. I shall discuss some of the weapons he used in subsequent chapters. Here it is enough to say that after devoting the best years of his life to implementing his Plan, he was exhausted, ill, and deeply depressed by a premonition of the American Revolution, a prospect that he laboured mightily to prevent and mercifully did not live to see. His letter to Andrew Eliot, just quoted, went on to say,

Now, a new Parlament [*sic*] having been chosen, my own affairs in the Country requiring personal inspection and attendance, my Constitution faltering, & being all over grey-pated, it is necessary that Retreat should take place. Doubt not, however, Dear Sir, that the Old Age of my Life will pass 'inactive, useless, insipid' when the leading Maxim of it will prove, I trust in God, OTIVM CVM DIGNITATE, which, in my humble station, I render, *Leasure with decorum*.

In the event he struggled on in London for two more years, and did not retreat to Dorset until the middle of 1770. A year later, on 29 May 1771, he wrote to his cousin Timothy that he had pursued 'a too rigorous Plan of private Patriotic action',[1] and had withdrawn almost entirely from the political arena.

There seems little reason to doubt that he had returned to England in 1753 with his goals already well defined, needing only to regain control of his own affairs before setting out on his course of action. He considered himself now a 'Citizen of the World', a phrase he was fond of inscribing on the flyleaves of books he presented anonymously; he was convinced that English government at its best provided the finest examples for other nations to follow; and he was determined to work for

[1] Harvard, MS Eng 1191.1.

19

the preservation and strengthening of civil and religious liberty at home and abroad – Roman Catholicism always excepted, but only if it attempted to interfere with civil government. This was Hollis's republicanism, closely coinciding with the classical Old Whig stance of his hero Molesworth, to whom I shall return. Into the implementation of his Plan he threw most of his time and all of his energy. A glance at the man himself will show that this energy was of no mean order.

Cipriani gave Blackburne an artist's description of Thomas Hollis in the prime of life:

He was over six feet tall, Herculean in size and strength, with a round face, low prominent forehead, bright brown eyes, high cheek bones, short nose, laughing mouth, and short neck, wide in the chest and shoulders. The rest of his body was similarly proportioned, and his knees and calves, which current fashion leaves uncovered, were perfect in their beauty, their shape and curves, and in keeping with his Herculean character; with all this there wonderfully joined an incomparable manner of gentleness and sweetness.[1]

Obviously in physical proportions alone such a man stood out from the crowd of his generally smaller contemporaries. Cipriani's words may be taken in conjunction with some of the portraits that have survived, beginning with the miniature ivory bas-relief by Andrea Pozzi dated Rome, 14 April 1752 – another birthday commemoration – which contrasts Hollis's robust physique with the more delicate build of his travelling companion, Thomas Brand.[2] The miniature, depicting Hollis bare-chested and bare-headed, contrasts amusingly with Richard Wilson's oil portrait of the same year, in which he appears elegantly dressed and bewigged. A fine portrait bust in marble in the Roman style by Joseph Wilton, of the later London period, also suggests his powerful physique, and on its socle it bears some of his favourite symbols of liberty (a liberty-cap flanked by two short swords) derived by Hollis from a coin of Marcus Brutus.[3] A somewhat primitive genre picture by John Green now hangs in the reading-room of the Houghton Library, depicting Hollis at one of his regular exercises with his London

[1] Cipriani's original Italian is printed in *Memoirs*, p. 503. I am indebted to Mrs Mollie Della Terza for the English translation.
[2] The ivories are in the Houghton Library, Harvard University, with another (possibly by the same hand) of one of Hollis's philosophical heroes, Francis Hutcheson (1694–1746). On the oil portrait by Richard Wilson, see note 3 p. 12 above; on two presumed likenesses by Canaletto, see note 1 p. 14 above.
[3] The bust is in the possession of the firm of Cyril Humphris, London. I am indebted to Mr Humphris for an opportunity to examine the sculpture at length, and for permission to reproduce a photograph of it.

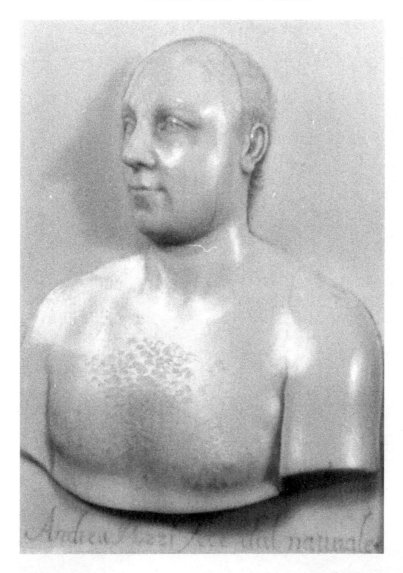

2   Miniature ivory bas-relief of Thomas Hollis by Andrea Pozzi, Rome, 1752

3   Marble bust of Thomas Hollis by Joseph Wilton, *c.* 1765

fencing-masters, the Martins, father and son. Finally there is the fine double portrait, first drawn and then engraved by Cipriani in the subject's forty-seventh year, at least partly to satisfy repeated requests from the President and Fellows of Harvard College, who wanted a likeness of their generous benefactor.[1]

I will not dwell on all the details of this familiar picture, but I should point out that Hollis is first depicted as a Roman and then, somewhat mischievously, in eighteenth-century wig and dress smiling benevolently in the lower right corner. In neither guise does he appear as Johnson described him, a 'poor, dull creature'. As a Roman he is surrounded by an array of his favourite symbols, many of which also appear on his bookbindings: the owl with a palm branch; the swords and liberty-cap, arranged as they are on Wilton's bust; the olive branch; and the seated Britannia with trident, shield, and liberty-pole. Although Hollis objected to the flaunting of oak-leaves on Oak-Apple Day, 29 May, because of the allusion to Charles II, otherwise they remained a favourite symbol of England for him, and they are prominent as in so many of his liberty-prints.

The theme of Marcus Brutus, suggested by the daggers and cap, is echoed below in a long passage that he selected from Plutarch's life of Brutus, of which the operative part is the remark ascribed to Messala when asked why he had fought against Octavius Caesar at Philippi but for him at Actium: 'I ever loved', said he, 'to take the best and justest part.' That is North's translation. In English, Greek, or Latin that suited Hollis as a motto, though I am not aware that he used it elsewhere.

Hollis's autograph diary from 14 April 1759 to 3 July 1770 is preserved in the Houghton Library.[2] Much of it is tantalizingly allusive, intended mainly as an *aide-mémoire*. He generally contented himself with recording the places he went to and the persons he met without much comment on conversations or actions; all the more tantalizing because most individuals are referred to by last name only. Yet many can be positively identified, and there are numerous though scattered passages describing conversations and encounters in some detail. He was an indefatigable pedestrian, walking the streets and lanes on both sides of the river in all weathers, and a great frequenter of coffee houses and taverns (though his customary fare seems to have been tea and toast).

[1] The original drawing (which did not include the inscription) is Harvard MS Typ 576 (31). Cipriani's engraving from his own drawing provides one of the frontispieces for Blackburne's *Memoirs*.　　[2] Harvard, MS Eng 1191.

His itineraries alone tell us much about his daily life in London – another reason for lamenting the loss of his travel diaries.

For a decade or more he faithfully attended the meetings of his learned societies, and in one of them, the Society for the Promotion of Arts, Manufactures, and Commerce,[1] he also attended many committee meetings, chairing a few of them. He was active in numerous public charities, both short-term such as the Committee for the Relief of French Prisoners of War, and permanent foundations: he was a Governor of both Guy's and St Thomas's Hospitals, and Guardian of the Asylum and the Magdalen Hospital. He also contributed generously to Hanway's Marine Society. In other words, his efforts and his benevolence were by no means restricted to the plan of life he had devised for himself.

Nor did he focus his energies on his plan to the exclusion of all recreation. The 'incomparable manner of gentleness and sweetness' of which Cipriani wrote was combined with a variety of recreations, a wide-ranging curiosity, a quiet sense of fun, and an appreciation of art and music. He kept a saddle-horse in a livery stable near Hyde Park Corner, and on many clement Sundays he rode to Esher for lunch, returning in time for a late tea at a neighbouring tavern. On several occasions he took a tour of a week or so, by coach and on horseback, to view the country seats of peers and gentlemen, and comment on their grounds, their mansions, and the collections they housed. He was never tempted to return to the continent.

He appears to have been as fond of the splendours of Ranelagh as was Dr Johnson; the diary records at least a dozen visits with various companions, and one of the paintings he commissioned from Canaletto depicts its Rotunda. He did not attend the theatre often, but he found the antics of Samuel Foote sufficiently amusing to return for them several times. He cast a critical eye on the art exhibitions staged at the Society for the Promotion of Arts, and when quarrels among the exhibitors resulted in the schism that eventually produced the Royal Academy and multiple exhibitions, he viewed them all not once but several times, and impartially disparaged what was on display. On the other hand, he collected contemporary paintings that were to his taste. The only concerts he mentions attending were six or eight performances

[1] Also called 'The Society for the Encouragement. . . [etc.]'. Hollis habitually used the name given in this text, and abbreviated it 'SPAC', which was also the abbreviation employed on the Hollis–Stuart medals, so I have adopted it here. It is now best known as the Royal Society of Arts.

4 Engraved double portrait of Thomas Hollis by Giovanni Battista Cipriani, 1767

of oratorios; he heard the *Messiah* twice, but was not enchanted by the rendition either time, and admittedly went on one occasion mostly to see George III and his consort in the royal box. But privately he was devoted to the flute, taking lessons from William DeFesch and sometimes playing in chamber ensemble with him and others. After a particularly trying day he often played the flute in solitude as a restorative before going to bed.

Many quiet evenings were devoted to reading, but except for one mention of *Candide*, which he hardly believed could have been written by Voltaire, there is little direct evidence of what he read. He shared Milton's low opinion of romances in general, and in the margin of a copy of Baron's edition (1756) of the second edition of *Eikonoklastes* he singled out Richardson's novels for special scorn.[1] Whether he paid any attention to the novels of Fielding, Sterne, Goldsmith, and Smollett does not appear. He freely quoted Shakespearian tags, and his frequent use of passages from *Paradise Lost, Paradise Regained, Samson Agonistes, Comus,* and the sonnets attests to his familiarity with Milton's verse as well as his prose. On occasion he showed at least passing acquaintance with Pope's *Essay on Man.* As noted earlier, he obviously admired the poems of Mark Akenside (to whom he presented the bed in which Milton was said to have died); he gave to the city of Bern the second edition of Richard Glover's *London, or the Progress of Commerce* (London 1739) in a fine emblematic binding, and gave its author a copy of his edition of Sidney's *Discourses Concerning Government* (1763); and he helped the publisher Andrew Millar to compose a suitable epitaph for James Thomson, so one assumes he knew Thomson's works. He appears to have been well read in Italian and in the Latin classics, and possibly in Greek. But it is probable that much of his later reading was in British and American journals, to keep up with current affairs, and in the prolific literature of political and religious controversy. What he read, he tended to annotate: his copy of the second edition of John Brown's *Estimate. . . of the Times* (London 1757)[2] is typical of many books thick with his marginalia. Evenings and sometimes whole days were devoted to correspondence, to preparing books for binding and distribution, and to editing or proofreading the texts he sponsored; others were spent arranging and listing his own collections.

Despite the private and solitary nature of much of Hollis's life, in the

---

[1] Harvard, x 27.20.5*.

[2] Harvard, *EC75.H7267.zz757b, not part of Hollis's gift; it was presented to Harvard in 1921 by John Woodbury of Boston. It lacks title and preliminaries, and its earlier provenance is not recorded. Perhaps Hollis sent it to Jonathan Mayhew or Andrew Eliot.

relatively small metropolis he came to know and to be known by many of its inhabitants, both prominent and obscure. His *Diary*, though requiring expansion and interpretation, reveals London life at many levels; for example, Hollis's frequent dealings with journalists, publishers, bookbinders, booksellers, graphic artists, numismatists, and antiquaries provide a great deal of new information.

He certainly rubbed elbows with an amazing array of literary, artistic, mercantile, and political Londoners in every social stratum; artists, artisans, and craftsmen; and interesting foreign visitors, many reappearing from his years on the continent. I will drop only a few names: Goldsmith, Sterne, Johnson, Mason, Gray, and Horace Walpole; Reynolds, Hogarth, Cipriani, Bartolozzi, Basire, Wilton, and Nollekens; Joseph Ames, the prototype of English bibliographers; Mr Justice Fielding, Mr Serjeant Nares, and Mr Speaker Onslow; Wilkes, Pitt the elder, and Pitt the younger; Archbishop Thomas Secker, with whom he was on familiar terms until Secker attacked Blackburne's book, *The Confessional*, and threatened to establish an episcopate in the New England colonies; a large assortment of prominent Dissenting divines, though he remarked that he was 'almost without any thing in common with the generality of dissenters, except in name'; and many eminent or well-informed persons in the American colonies, such as Jonathan Mayhew, Andrew Eliot, Harrison Gray, Israel and Jasper Mauduit, Benjamin Franklin, and John Adams. His influence was enough to gain him a private interview on 23 October 1765 with the Marquis of Rockingham, then Prime Minister, to transmit the alarm and objection of the New England colonists regarding the Stamp Act, though his eloquence left the Marquis unmoved; Hollis sadly recorded the Minister's dusty answer and concluded, 'My little Power of action among the Great. . . has however been faithfully exerted.'

A man with so many and such prominent contacts remains obscure only by design and strategy, and so it was with Hollis, the anonymous republican. His strategies themselves came to breach his anonymity. Any sumptuously bound volume inscribed to the recipient by 'an Englishman, a Lover of Liberty, the Principles of the Revolution & the Protestant Succession in the House of Hanover, Citizen of the World', was all too readily identified as coming from Hollis. Thus Horace Walpole responded next day to the gift of a volume so inscribed by giving in return a handsome volume from the Strawberry Hill Press.[1]

[1] Most of Hollis's gifts to Walpole are now in the Pierpont Morgan Library; see Allen T. Hazen *A Catalogue of Horace Walpole's Library* (New Haven 1969), nos. 1694, 2647, 2730, 2775, 3172, and 3176. In response to the inscribed gift of no. 3176, Sidney's *Discourses*

Walpole, a much more tepid Whig than Hollis, was inclined to make fun of his efforts at propaganda and his radical (or Old Whig) position. Hollis found the purest essence of congenial political philosophy in Robert Molesworth's introduction to his translation of François Hotman's *Franco-Gallia*, an introduction deemed unwise to publish during the reign of Queen Anne, but safely added in the second edition of 1721. Molesworth believed in the interdependence of three estates, the Sovereign, the Lords, and the Commons, responsible to one another, and in the right of the Commons to take what action might be necessary should the Sovereign or other executive violate the contract. This he proudly called a Commonwealth, differentiating this use of the word from its application in Cromwellian times, when it had gradually deteriorated into its own kind of tyranny. He believed in religious tolerance, with the proviso that religion should not attempt to tamper with government; in frequent parliaments with election by ballot, in which the chosen representatives would have to be property-holders to ensure that their interests ran with the electorate; in a general naturalization to attract talent from other lands; and in arming and training the freeholders for mutual defence, while he opposed maintaining a standing army in time of peace. In embracing Molesworth's philosophy, Hollis was clearly declaring for a republic rather than a democracy. The benevolent rule of an intellectual élite, in his view, was the surest means of preserving and fostering his ideals of civil and religious liberty; as he wrote to the Reverend Andrew Eliot on 1 July 1768, 'In the Energic Minds of A FEW, not in numbers, doth the safety, felicity of states depend.'[1]

Molesworth's principles were certainly not original, though forcefully put. Many persons earlier and later shared similar ideas, as did Hollis, who thought that Molesworth's was their most eloquent statement. Complaints stemming from such ideas are prominent among the twenty-six charges that the central portion of the Declaration of Independence levelled at the no doubt astonished George III, who was

---

Concerning Government (London 1763), Walpole gave Hollis the Strawberry Hill Lucan; to no. 3172, Locke's *Letters Concerning Toleration* (London 1765), which contained no presentation inscription but displayed the emblematic tools on the binding, Walpole replied at once with the Strawberry Hill *Life* of Lord Herbert of Cherbury, a copy now in the Grenville Collection, British Library.

[1] Original in the Hollis Papers, Massachusetts Historical Society. Much the same sentiments appear in other letters to Edmund Quincy, Jr, 1 October 1766, and Andrew Eliot, 10 May 1769.

surely innocent of many of them.[1] Hollis did not live to see that document, but long before his death he heard such sentiments echoing from the colonies, not only on the North American continent but also in the West Indies. As the British government and the colonists came more and more into conflict, Hollis grew correspondingly more distressed; as Secker and the Society for the Propagation of the Gospel seemed more and more bent on an unwelcome episcopal establishment in North America, he raised his voice, albeit anonymously, in protest; and he followed every move on both sides of the Atlantic, reading the Boston press in almost daily visits to the New England Coffee House, talking to American visitors there and elsewhere, and sometimes even going among the traders lying at anchor in the Thames to collect the latest intelligence.

Such activities were merely preliminary to achieving the goals of his private plan: to foster and extend human liberty, to eliminate governmental corruption, and to establish religious toleration, even extending, with certain safeguards, to Roman Catholics.[2]

How he set about implementing his plan must be inferred from all kinds of fragmentary evidence, but there is a lot of it, much of which will appear in more detail presently. It involved financing printers and publishers in the production of what Professor Caroline Robbins has called his 'canonical books', as well as other texts;[3] rewarding the publishers of periodicals for 'services to liberty' in the printing of letters and articles; the design and calculated distribution of symbolic medals, prints, and bookbindings; and the enlistment of like-minded writers and preachers to spread the word.

---

[1] See Howard Mumford Jones 'The Declaration of Independence: A Critique' *Proceedings of the American Antiquarian Society* 85 (1975), pp. 55–72, esp. 59–62.

[2] In 1767 Caleb Fleming originated a 'Plan for Preventing the Growth of Popery in England', subsequently much revised with Hollis's help. Fleming's first draft was harsh and even bloodthirsty: for example, Popish priests were to be licensed, and the penalty for an unlicensed priest who performed priestly offices publicly or privately was the loss of the fourth finger on the right hand; a second violation constituted a capital offence. Over a period of months, Hollis evidently succeeded in softening the proposal considerably, and that penalty was reduced simply to prescribing that unlicensed priests could not reside in the kingdom. The process of modification can be seen in successive drafts published in the *London Chronicle* over the signature of 'A Lover of his King and Country' on 22–4 January, 16–18 April, 30 July–1 August, and 3–6 October 1767. Its final form is printed in *Memoirs*, pp. 706–8.

[3] Robbins 'Library of Liberty – Assembled for Harvard College by Thomas Hollis of Lincoln's Inn' *Harvard Library Bulletin* 5 (1951), pp. 5–23, 185–96, esp. pp. 188–96; reprinted (inexplicably without the list of books) in her *Absolute Liberty* ed. Barbara Taft ([Hamden, Connecticut] 1982), pp. 226–9.

Despite all precautions, the scale of his operations was so extensive and they went on so long that he clearly became notorious. Almost certainly he was an object of suspicion to the Tory government, from his association with radical politicians like Wilkes and incendiary publishers like John Almon and George Kearsley, from the nature of the texts that he caused to be reprinted, and from their wide distribution. This may explain a phenomenon that has troubled readers of his *Diary*, including his first biographer, Blackburne: his obsession during his later years in London that he was continually watched and followed by spies and *agents provocateurs*. He was convinced that these persons were Roman Catholic agents, that they tampered with his mail and infiltrated his household and the establishments of printers and binders whom he employed, and that one of their aims was to provoke a street brawl in which he might be injured or even killed. 'But I shall know how to defend myself', he stoutly declared, and he regularly took the *parades* with his fencing-master, which is the science of parrying rather than the art of attack. Fearing that he might not be believed, Hollis invited several of his friends (among them, William Strahan, Jr) to visit his house and observe these persecutions, and they do not appear to have contradicted him.

Nevertheless, Blackburne, among others, took this as evidence of a breakdown brought on by severe mental and physical strain, and he played it down in the *Memoirs* as a kind of unfortunate manifestation. But Professor Betty Rizzo has ingeniously suggested[1] that at least some of the spies were real, and that they were governmental, not Roman Catholic. Little is known and few records exist of the activities of the Secret Service employed by the Secretaries of State to watch the movements of suspicious radicals or political opponents, and nothing involving surveillance of Hollis. There is a rare survival in the *Grenville Papers*[2] of detailed reports on the daily and hourly movements of John Wilkes and his allies during two weeks of November 1763. It may well be that Hollis was subjected to the same kind of attention, and simply mistook the source of his persecution and exaggerated its extent. Anonymous though he tried to be, he was physically conspicuous. He walked all over London and its environs in all weathers during long days, he dined and drank tea in sundry taverns and coffee-houses (some with notorious political and Masonic connections, though that does not seem to have been the reason for his choosing them), he engaged in all

---

[1] In correspondence with the author.
[2] Ed. William James Smith (London 1852) 2, pp. 155–60.

sorts of mysterious business with printers, publishers, writers, book-sellers, journalists, and Dissenting ministers. He was also gathering and shipping large numbers of possibly seditious publications to that potential hotbed of political unrest, Harvard College, whose library collection he undertook to rebuild after its disastrous fire in 1764. That is another chapter to be taken up later. He was obviously someone who would bear watching by ministers hostile to his views and not always secure in their position.

All this is interesting speculation, but the fact is that by 1770 Hollis had worn himself out in the cause and felt he could do little more. In July he left London for his beloved Dorset, where he found renewed energy in putting his farms in order, in dealing (mostly at long range) with the charitable trusts for which he shared responsibility with cousin Timothy, and in renewing acquaintance with an old hero, Pitt the elder, then in retirement at Burton Pynsent nearby. Hollis had forgiven him for the sin of accepting an earldom at the hands of Bute. Letters of both Hollis and Chatham paint a charming picture of Hollis's relations with the Pitt family, and especially with William Pitt the younger, with whom he engaged in long philosophical conversations.[1]

Meantime he continued to lease the house in Pall Mall where he had lived for many years, on the easterly of the two small streets that provide a link with St James's Square, to use on his occasional visits to London. It is probable that he kept most of his collections there. In the country, Hollis often stayed in the farmhouse at Urles Farm, one of his properties, although in various ways he felt it inadequate for his needs; but, despite constant searching, he found nothing better. In Lyme he maintained a suite of rooms in one of the principal inns, the Three Cups, which he owned – exactly when he purchased it is not clear. Characteristically, he called his suite 'Liberty Hall' and so designated it in a sign over the door. When Chatham visited Lyme at Hollis's invitation, he too was put up at the Three Cups.

Hollis's benevolence now extended to the town of Lyme. As usual he rejoiced in good works for the benefit of those around him. He purchased from the Henley family, then Lords of the Manor of Lyme, a property known as the Cobham Warehouses, hitherto leased by various merchants. This he presented to the Corporation of Lyme in 1773, and

---

[1] *Memoirs*, p. 481; Caroline Robbins 'Thomas Hollis in His Dorsetshire Retirement' *Harvard Library Bulletin* 23 (1975), pp. 411–28, reprinted in *Absolute Liberty* cited above, pp. 230–46. See also John Hutchins *The History and Antiquities of Dorset* 3d ed. (Westminster 1863) 3, pp. 91, 96–9.

the building was converted into the Assembly Rooms, a necessary amenity in any respectable watering-place. It survived into the twentieth century and eventually became a cinema. He also purchased and presented to the town, so that it might be pulled down, a row of dilapidated tenements that blocked the end of a principal street, and bought and pulled down another similar property that was an eyesore and beyond redemption.[1]

But his principal attention was directed towards the farms he had acquired years earlier. Their crops and their cattle came under his personal supervision. They provide evidence that his patriotic fervour was unabated, though flowing in new channels. With one or two exceptions he gave his farms names to suit his republican fancy: Harrington, Milton, Sidney, Ludlow, Neville, Locke, Harvard, Marvell, Liberty, Buchanan, and Russell. During most of 1773 he devoted much time and thought to this nomenclature, which extended even to the individual fields. To this day most of Hollis's estates bear the names he gave them: Harvard Farm near Halstock has fields still called New England, Boston, Mayhew, Cotton, Eliot, Adams, Revolution, and Massachusetts, and a copse that has always resisted tilling and is called Stuart; Liberty Farm nearby has fields called Confucius, Lycurgus, Solon, Socrates, and the like. He called this 'patriotizing' his properties.[2] He continued to write occasional notes for the London journals and to correspond with his friends, though less frequently, and he saw

[1] C. Wanklyn *Lyme Regis, a Retrospect* (London 1927), pp. 114–17, 205–8; George Roberts *The History of Lyme-Regis* (Sherborne 1823), pp. 195–7; Dorothy Gardiner *Companion into Dorset* (London [1937]), pp. 93–6, 155–6, and (on one of Robert Thorner's charities) 160; John Fowles *A Short History of Lyme Regis* (Boston 1982), pp. 28–9. Fowles states, contrary to other sources, that Hollis merely rented rooms in the Three Cups, and says that in 1771 'he bought land by the shore and. . . created the first public promenade there – today the eastern end of Marine Parade (a crass municipal name for what many in Lyme still call by its Regency one – the Walk)'.

[2] A detailed survey of the properties was drawn up by John Doyley in 1799 for Brand Hollis, and is preserved in the Dorset County Archives, Dorchester; I am indebted to Professor Robbins for a photocopy. On the naming of farms and fields, see Robbins, note 1 p. 31 above; Pam Lemmey 'A North Dorset Farm: Liberty Farm, Halstock' in *History from the Farm* ed. William George Hoskins (London [1970]), pp. 51–6; W. H. Bond 'Assertor of Liberty, Citizen of the World' *Harvard Magazine* (March 1974), pp. 33–5, on Harvard Farm. See Ordnance Survey maps, one-inch series, sheets 177 and 178, on which several of the farms are marked by name. A curious foreshadowing of this 'patriotizing' appears in *Diary* 31 October 1765–30 March 1770 *passim*, when Hollis records his habit of cashing draughts on his account at Messrs Hoare drawn to the order of 'Marchamont Nedham or bearer', 'Marcus Brutus or bearer', 'Mutius Scaevola or bearer', and the like.

through the press and caused to be appropriately bound an edition of Algernon Sidney's *Works* (London 1772); but he kept no diary.

On 1 January 1774, as Hollis was walking among his fields with his workmen, he suddenly fell dead. In the phrase from Milton's second sonnet to Cyriack Skinner, which Hollis had paraphrased in speaking of the death of Jonathan Mayhew, he had been 'overply'd in liberty's defence'.

As Blackburne described it in 1780, 'In the middle of one of these fields, not far from his house [at Urles Farm], he ordered his corpse to be deposited in a grave ten feet deep, and that the field should be plowed over, that no trace of his burial-place might remain.'[1] He was determined to be anonymous to the end.

But even this last attempt at anonymity was partially foiled. *The Gentleman's Magazine* for January 1774 – the same issue that reported, with some sympathy for the colonists, the affair known as the Boston Tea Party – recorded Hollis's burial at Corscombe, with a brief but eloquent obituary:

This gentleman was formed on the severe but exalted plan of antient Greece, in whom was united the humane and disinterested virtue of Brutus, and the active and determined spirit of Sidney; illustrious in his manner of using ample fortune, not by spending it in the parade of life, which he despised, but by assisting the deserving, and encouraging the Arts and Sciences, which he promoted with zeal and affection, knowing the love of them leads to moral and intellectual beauty; was a warm and strenuous advocate in the cause of public liberty and virtue, and for the rights of human nature and private conscience. His humanity and generosity were not confined to the small spot of his own country; he sought for merit in every part of the globe, considering himself as a citizen of the world, but concealed his acts of munificence, being contented with the consciousness of having done well. Posterity will look up with admiration to this great Man, who, like Milton, is not sufficiently known by this degenerate age in which he lived, tho' it will have cause to lament the loss of him.

Men are not immortalized by their burial-places, but 'Che trae l'uom del Sepolcro, ed in vita il serba'. Thomas Hollis of Lincoln's Inn, Assertor of Liberty, Citizen of the World, is to be remembered among patriots with respect, and among libraries and their users with affectionate veneration, nowhere more than at Harvard College: in the words of his own favourite quotation from *Paradise Regained*, 'By deeds of peace'.

---

[1] *Memoirs*, p. 481.

2

Hollis's bindings

WHEN JAMES BOSWELL rewrote the account in his journal of Mrs Garrick's dinner-party (1781) and incorporated it in the *Life of Johnson*, he added a passage identifying Thomas Hollis as 'the strenuous Whig, who used to send over Europe presents of democratical books, with their boards stamped with daggers and caps of liberty'.[1] Here he harked back to a much earlier part of his journal, when he travelled in Switzerland and took pains to make the acquaintance of such eminences as Voltaire and Rousseau. On 30 November 1764, he visited Bern:

I must here remark that in this and all the principal Librarys that I have seen abroad, they have shewn me a present of Books sent them by a certain unknown whimsical Englishman. He is no doubt a most prodigious Whig, for he has sent Milton's Prose Works (which I suppose he preferrs to his Poetry), Toland's *life of Milton*, Algernon Sydney's works, and several other such dainty pieces of British Republican Writing. The Books are bound in red Morocco, and adorned with gilded Stamps of the Cap of Liberty, Pitch-forks, Swords, and I know not what other terrible Instruments of fury. I am surprised that he has not thought of introducing the Scaffold, the Block and the Ax. He might have adorned a whole Board with a Representation of the Murder of King Charles. He has, however, a stamp of Great-Britain, as she is usually seen pourtrayed upon Our halfpence; to render her, however, compleat, he has subjoined this sensible and sublime Inscription, '*O Fair Britannia! hail!*' Lest Sydney, Milton and Toland should not be strong enough in the good cause, our Enthusiast has now and then added notes of his own, and quotations from others like himself. He has taken care to copy an apt Passage in the Poetry of Mr. Richard Glover. In short he has made me laugh very heartily.[2]

Though Boswell found Hollis's books laughable in 1764 and spoke of them patronizingly in 1781, they clearly made a considerable impression on him. Not only did he unconsciously prove the validity of an important element in Hollis's plan, he eventually adopted a version of Hollis's liberty-cap for the bindings of his own works favouring Paoli and promoting freedom for the Corsicans. It must also be pointed out

[1] Ed. Hill and Powell 4, p. 97.
[2] *Boswell with Rousseau and Voltaire 1764* ed. Geoffrey Steele and Frederick Pottle (privately printed 1928), pp. 46–7, in *Private Papers of James Boswell 4*.

that Boswell failed utterly to recognize the classical antecedents of Hollis's symbols, mistaking Neptune's trident for a pitchfork, and conveniently overlooking emblems of peace and prosperity.[1]

Hollis was not perversely eccentric or indulging in ostentation in commissioning his symbolic bindings and distributing them so widely and purposefully. As he himself wrote to President Edward Holyoke of Harvard on 24 June 1765:

> The bindings of Books are little regarded by me for my own proper library; but by long experience I have found it necessary to attend to them for other libraries, having thereby drawn notice, with preservation, on many excellent books, or curious, which, it is probable, would else have passed unheeded or neglected.[2]

The proof lies in the extraordinarily large number of Hollis bindings that have survived, in the interest that they have always invited, and in the influence sometimes exerted by the texts they contain.

There seems to be a paradox in the fact that many of the finest Hollis bindings still extant were indeed in Hollis's own library, from which they emerged in the Disney sale in 1817;[3] but he had been an inveterate collector since his days in Italy if not earlier, and he appreciated fine printing and binding as much as anyone. The unpublished context in his letter to Holyoke shows that he was being politely and modestly self-deprecating, for he was thanking the Harvard President for the gift of a copy of Nathaniel Appleton's sermon on the death of Edward Wigglesworth, the first Hollis Professor of Divinity at Harvard, bound (as Holyoke had written on 11 May 1765), 'as neatly . . . as we cou'd'.[4] Hollis simply felt that Holyoke should not have to apologize for a colonial binding that was less sophisticated than those produced by

---

[1] Boswell was also mistaken in questioning Hollis's familiarity with Milton's poetry.

[2] *Memoirs*, p. 603.

[3] *Catalogue of the. . . United Libraries of Thomas Hollis, Esq. and Thomas Brand Hollis, Esq. . . . Including the. . . Library of the Late Rev. John Disney* Sotheby (London, 22 April 1817), copy with prices and buyers in the Houghton Library. Many of the finest bindings were acquired by Richard Heber, and passed from his collection to that of Sir George Holford, from which they were later dispersed.

[4] Nathaniel Appleton *Discourse Occasioned by the Death of Dr. Wigglesworth* (Boston 1765); 1817 sale catalogue, lot 40, 6d. to Hunter; present location unknown. Holyoke's letter is preserved in the Hollis Papers, Massachusetts Historical Society. A copy of the book was presented to Harvard by Wigglesworth's son and namesake, the second Hollis Professor of Divinity (*AC7.Ap552.765f), in a mourning binding by Andrew Barclay of Boston, Mass., a rather provincial imitation of the style of a number of London bindings executed for Hollis and sent by him to the College. Without much doubt a similarly bound copy evoked Hollis's letter to Holyoke concerning the binding of books.

London craftsmen such as Richard Montagu, John Matthewman, and John Shove, the men he himself most often employed.[1]

Authors have had books put into special bindings to attract patronage, and bibliophiles have caused emblems and mottoes to be stamped on their bindings, often accompanied by far more ornate decorations, but usually for their personal libraries, sometimes for special presentation, but seldom if ever for distribution on such a scale. Their supra-libros stamps were much more likely to be heraldic or otherwise to proclaim ownership, with an occasional pious note that their books were also intended for the use of their friends. Hollis is unique in the large number of emblems he employed, the care with which he chose them, and the generosity with which he commissioned such bindings in order to scatter them far and wide.

All his emblems appear to have had specific significance for him. Unfortunately he left no key to their meaning. Some are sufficiently obvious, but others remain obscure. Clues in his diary and correspondence, in the sources on which he apparently drew, in the original drawings that survive for many of the tools, and in the nature of the texts on which he caused them to be stamped, can provide a clearer understanding of most of them. The emblems also appear in, and add meaning to, the 'liberty-prints' he commissioned various artists to draw and engrave for wide distribution, but all of these are later in date than the binders' tools. The eighteenth century was still sensitive to the value of emblems, and Hollis could count on the fact that many observers would not be as obtuse as Boswell in understanding them.

By no means all of the bindings commissioned by Hollis bore emblematic tools, which he reserved to draw 'notice, with preservation' to his liberty texts and to other works that he particularly admired. Obviously he believed that any book worth preserving was worth a sound binding. The majority of those sent to Harvard, and many sent to other libraries and individuals, were relatively plain or were decorated with designs made up of ordinary *petits fers*, though sometimes employed in unusual ways. Both emblematic and non-emblematic bindings share certain characteristics that closely link them, and they also use tools and

---

[1] Ellic Howe *A List of London Bookbinders* (London 1950). On Montagu, pp. 69 and xxxv; like many other writers, Howe does not distinguish clearly between Montagu's bindings and those done by others for Hollis. On Matthewman (consistently spelled 'Mathewman' in Hollis's *Diary*), p. 67, but without recording his first name, his partnership with John Bailey, and much other pertinent information. On Shove, also without his first name, p. 85.

shop practices that should eventually differentiate the binders of the non-symbolic bindings, although this problem must be reserved for another study. Identification is further complicated by the fact that many of the non-emblematic tools and rolls are of common design, identical to or closely resembling those employed by numerous contemporary binders.

With the exception of a number of symbolic bindings executed by Matthewman, the spines bear leather labels or lettering-pieces of different colour from the binding, with sometimes idiosyncratic identifications stamped in gold capitals, using individual tools rather than letters set in a pallet. The words of the title are usually set off in the manner of classical inscriptions by full stops at the level of hyphens. The endpapers are almost invariably marbled in either of two principal styles, the bold swirls of the 'common' French marbling, or the much smaller Dutch combed designs, each represented by at least four sub-varieties;[1] one cannot be more specific, because every sheet of marbled paper is necessarily unique, and the varieties tend to merge into one another. Most are in the conventional combination of red, blue, yellow, and green on a white background, but occasionally unusual pastel colours appear. In most volumes the end-leaves are sewn in, the stitches showing plainly in the inner hinges. Single leaves of marbled paper are sometimes used as dividers in tract volumes. A few publications, possibly deemed by Hollis to be ephemeral, were simply covered with wrappers of one of his typical marbled papers. The only ones so treated that have been located at Harvard are the annual pamphlets of rules, members, and premiums of the SPAC (now the Royal Society of Arts).

The edges of the leaves are most often finely sprinkled in red and polished. In a few special books they are marbled more or less to match the endpapers, showing that while most marbled paper at that period was imported, English binders could execute marbling when they needed to. In a few exceptional cases all three edges are gilt, but top edges are never gilt by themselves. Despite having his books cut to produce smooth edges, Hollis was at pains to preserve margins as far as possible.

Almost without exception, the edges of the boards are decorated with a plain or dotted fillet or with one of a dozen or so ornamental rolls. They are of conventional design. A few are blind-stamped, but most are

---

[1] I am indebted to Mr Richard J. Wolfe for authoritative information about eighteenth-century marbling.

5 Marbled paper in the French style

6 Marbled paper in the Dutch style

gilt. The headbands are sewn in red and white, green and white, red and green, or red, green, and white; exceptions are few. They are usually worked over a thin strip of leather or a paper roll. Each volume has a dark green silk ribbon marker fastened at the middle of the top headband; a few thick volumes have more than one marker.

The books Hollis acquired during his Italian sojourn were mostly bound there in stiff vellum and not tampered with later; their edges are more coarsely sprinkled in red and green, their headbands are usually solid green, and they have a distinctive blue-green grosgrain ribbon marker quite different from the usual dark colour and smooth texture. They were, of course, sawed in. Most of the English bindings, however, have raised bands. Unless very small or very large, they were sewn on five cords. All were sewn with stout linen thread. Only Matthewman's octavo and duodecimo symbolic bindings have the cords sawed in to produce smooth spines; many of these also have titles lettered directly on the spine, rather than on lettering-pieces. The sewing in books that have been sawed in shows a regular pattern of skipping first one cord and then another, saving labour and also avoiding undue thickening of the spine.

The most frequent leathers are polished red sheep and morocco, but citron and green occasionally appear, and some emblematic bindings are in russia or in smooth brown calf. Most non-emblematic bindings are in polished calf, plain or sprinkled; a few, mostly tract volumes, in unfinished (or suede) calf; fewer still in sheep. I have seen only two emblematic bindings, both by Montagu, bound in vellum over stiff boards.[1] In several instances, Hollis had volumes bound in black mourning bindings with black end-leaves and black ribbon markers: his symbolism could extend to colour in order to emphasize events that he considered deplorable.[2]

Anomalies occur because of a practice that Hollis (and binders generally) called 'vamping'. Some books that he acquired were already

[1] One, in the possession of the present writer, contains four quarto pamphlets by Mark Akenside, all first editions, including *Odes on Several Subjects* (1745), from which Hollis derived the motto for his bindings. The other is in Stadt- und Universitätsbibliothek Bern, Hollis no. 261, John Locke *Two Treatises of Government* (London 1690).

[2] Such bindings occur on John Free's sermon *England's Warning Piece* (London [1768]) on the Massacre in St George's Fields, bound with his anniversary sermon of the next year (Harvard, *EC75.F8754.768ec) and a copy of the *Short Narrative of the Horrid Massacre* (Boston 1770) on the Boston Massacre, presented to Christ's College, Cambridge. Hollis sent Harvard a similarly bound copy of the London edition of the *Short Narrative* (1770) (*AC75.B6747.770sb), but it was rebound in library buckram in 1908 and only the black edges remain as evidence of the mourning binding.

in perfectly sound or even handsome bindings, and these he directed his binders to vamp by inserting new end-papers, new headbands, and the customary green silk ribbon markers. He might also have his emblematic tools added to the decoration and typical lettering-pieces applied to the spines, producing anachronistic blends of style that would seem puzzling but for the explanation of vamping.

A substantial number of the older books that Hollis ordered to be rebound occur with their title-pages closely trimmed to the edge of the letterpress and laid down on leaves of sound paper, a precaution taken, no doubt, to ensure the survival of original leaves that were fatigued or even damaged. He does not appear to have specified this practice unless he felt it was strictly necessary. One can also find examples of books in which the loss of a title-page or some other portion of the text has been supplied neatly (and evidently with some care to be accurate) in Hollis's unmistakable and very legible autograph.

Perhaps most striking of all, many of the books in emblematic bindings (except those by his earliest identifiable binder, Montagu) contain on the front and back binders' leaves, and sometimes elsewhere within the volume, smoke or carbon prints of the symbolic tools.[1] These are exactly like the smoke proofs taken by letter-cutters in following the progress of their work on typographical punches. The tool was held in a smoky flame and then carefully imprinted, probably while warm, on paper. An extraordinarily sharp and accurate image resulted. In a number of books a whole blank leaf bears an elaborate design made up of emblematic smoke prints. One book in stiff white vellum has a tool smoke-printed near the top of the spine, the only observed example of smoke-printing on the exterior of a volume, and unquestionably a case of vamping; but it would appear that Thomas Brand Hollis was responsible for this bit of decoration.[2]

Such details are worth recording because they do not represent standard shop practices, as they might in so many cases, but rather the close supervision of Hollis himself. His *Diary* contains many hints of which the entry for 30 April 1762 is one of the more specific: 'Employed in looking over divers parcels of books which I have lately purchased, and in sorting them, and writing directions concerning them for Shove and Mathewman.'

---

[1] Some writers have mistaken these for prints made with ink; examination under a lens shows that they are not.

[2] Celsus *De arte medici libri octo* ed. Guglielmo Pantini (Basle [1553]), Harvard, LC 31.115F*; the tool is the owl and palm (2b).

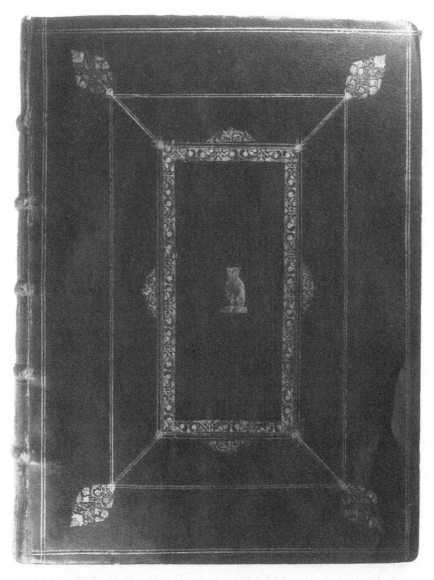

7   Early binding vamped by John Matthewman after 1764, the owl
(1b) added in a different gold-leaf (cover 23.7 × 18 cm)

Evidence survives to show how he conveyed his instructions. With pen and ink, on slips of paper about two inches wide and six or eight inches long, he specified the number of bands by drawing double horizontal lines for each band; he wrote, sometimes in capital letters, the text, line division, and punctuation of the lettering-pieces; and he added in his current hand such other instructions as he felt necessary, including which tools were to be smoke-printed inside the book. A slip for one of the plainer bindings was accidentally bound into a volume preserved at Bern,[1] and some seven or eight volumes at Harvard contain more or less legible offsets from the freshly written ink of exactly similar slips, readable at least in part with a mirror or through reversed photography. This method of conveying instructions was employed with Matthewman and Shove, the binders he used almost exclusively during the last decade and a half of his life; I have observed no example of such instructions directed to Montagu.

BINDINGS BY RICHARD MONTAGU

When Hollis began to carry out his plan of binding certain books in a striking manner in order to call attention to them and to ensure their preservation, it was natural for him to turn to Richard Montagu, an experienced craftsman whose shop was in Great Queen Street close to Lincoln's Inn Fields and not far from the rooms Hollis had occupied in the Inn. Montagu had been located there since 1728, so Hollis may have known of him even before setting out on his European travels, but I am aware of no identifiable bindings executed for him by Montagu that date from this early period.

Montagu's bindings for Hollis display many tools but only two designs appear to be used as emblems, and it seems likely that they were simply a part of his shop stock, rather than having been designed and cut especially for Hollis (see plate 10, where they are reproduced actual size). A ducally crowned lion statant gardant on a chapeau or cap-of-maintenance appears in two sizes: the vertical measurement of M2a is 25 mm, that of M2b is 18 mm. The larger lion can be seen to be gorged with a collar compony-counter compony (i.e., chequered); the other is too small to show such details. The lions occur only on the spines of books. This heraldic crest could not properly belong to Hollis. It may have

---

[1] In James Greenwood *An Essay towards a Practical English Grammar* (London 1753), Stadt- und Universitätsbibliothek Bern, Hollis no. 292.

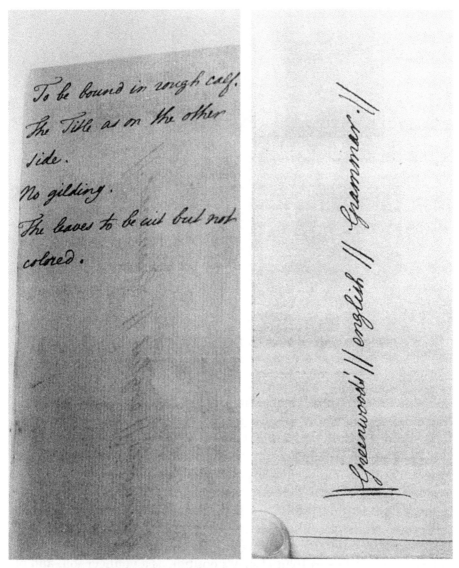

8–9 Hollis's directions to the binder, accidentally preserved in Bern Hollis 292; recto (left) and verso

MIa   MIb   MIc

M2a   M2b   M2c
                          (not Montagu:
                          Disney crest)

10   Emblems used on bindings by Richard Montagu, with the lion crest of the Reverend John Disney

pertained to Augustus Henry Fitzroy, 3rd Duke of Grafton, though there are several other possibilities.[1] Very likely Hollis chose it to represent the British lion without regard to precise heraldic usage.

The Reverend John Disney, who inherited the Hollis library on the death of Brand Hollis in 1804, introduced some confusion by adopting a supra-libros tool (usually employed on boards, not spines) cut for himself representing the Disney family crest: a lion statant gardant, bearing a crescent for difference, standing on a roll (shown as M2c). It is appreciably smaller than Montagu's M2b, measuring 12 mm in height. The crescent indicates John Disney's position as a younger son, and of course there is no ducal coronet. The same crest appears on Disney's engraved bookplate.[2] Since, as will be seen, Disney also inherited at least a few of the last set of Hollis's emblematic tools, it occasionally occurs in combination with one or more of them. He also appears to have added it

[1] James Fairbairn *Fairbairn's Book of Crests* 4th ed. (London 1905), plate 4 no. 2.
[2] Disney's lion is M2c in plate 10; although never used by Montagu, it is included with his tools for convenience and comparison. It is also reproduced with Disney's book-plate and cipher in plate 11.

44

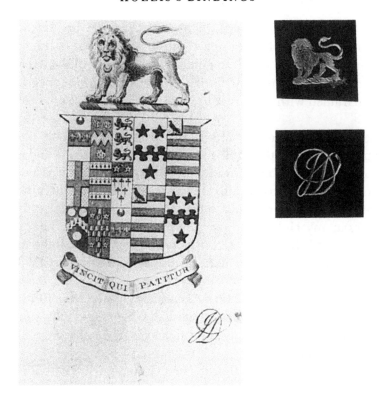

11 Bookplate, supra-libros crest (M2c) and monogram of the
Reverend John Disney (1746–1816)

to a few bindings done earlier for Hollis or Brand Hollis. Its superficial
likeness to Montagu's ducally crowned lion must be coincidence;
Disney was born in 1746 and therefore cannot have been more than
twelve or thirteen years old when Montagu was using the crowned lion
tools. Moreover, there appears to be no blood tie between the Disney
and Hollis families.

Montagu's other emblem is a standard and not particularly graceful
seated Britannia, cut in three sizes: the vertical measurement of M1a is 28
mm, of M1b 23 mm, and of M1c 17 mm. It is placed in the centre of the
front and back covers, the size determined by the dimensions of the
book. It also occurs on spines, where its size and that of the lion are
determined by the thickness of the volume. On texts that Hollis
particularly esteemed – the liberty texts of Sidney, Milton, Locke, and
Molesworth – the symbolism of Britannia was emphasized by surrounding her, on front and back covers, with a garland of oak leaves and the

motto, O FAIR BRITANNIA HAIL. The centres of the boards on these bindings are pierced almost imperceptibly by one foot of the compass used to trace circles, in blind, to guide the placement of the wreath and motto around the figure of Britannia. The covers of these special books were also framed with elaborate borders made up of *petits fers* (see plate 12).[1]

Other books bound for Hollis by Montagu bear the lion and Britannia tools, but with simple fillets bordering the covers and a star in each corner. In a number of examples, Volume 1 of Milton's *Prose Works* (London 1753–56) also contains elaborately tooled doublures including the smallest of the Britannia tools, the only observed examples of doublures in any Hollis bindings (see plates 13 and 14). That volume includes those of Milton's prose works most esteemed by Hollis and most often annotated by him; in none of these sets is the second volume decorated with doublures.

The motto is taken from Mark Akenside's eighth Ode, 'On Leaving Holland', already quoted at some length in Chapter 1; Hollis sometimes copied out several stanzas on the flyleaves of books he considered particularly noteworthy.

It seems more than likely that the first contemporary embodiment of one of his 'liberty texts' that Hollis encountered when he returned to England in 1753 was the monumental two-volume edition of Milton's *Prose Works* edited by Richard Baron and published in that same year, and a copy of it was the first emblematic binding that he sent to Harvard College in 1758. More copies of it than of any other book survive in Montagu bindings. (Hollis evidently put by some copies in sheets or boards, because the copies he gave to Göttingen and Stockholm in 1761–62 were bound by Matthewman using tools designed by Cipriani.)

As originally published, Baron's edition reprinted *Eikonoklastes* from the first edition of 1649. In 1755 Baron came upon the somewhat rarer second edition of 1650, previously unknown to him, containing

---

[1] Similar bindings by Montagu on Milton's *Prose Works* are in the library of Christ's College, Cambridge; Biblioteca Nazionale, Florence (see Howard M. Nixon *Five Centuries of English Bookbinding* (London [1978]), no. 67); Stadt- und Universitätsbibliothek Bern, Hollis no. 69, in diced russia; and no doubt elsewhere. Much later Jonas Hanway used a head of Britannia and Akenside's motto on presentation copies of his *Proposals for County Naval Free-Schools* ([London 1783]) and other emblematic tools on other volumes; see G. D. Hobson *English Bindings 1490–1940 from the Library of J. R. Abbey* (London 1940), pp. 120–4, Nixon, cited above, no. 78, and Maggs Bros. Ltd *Bookbinding in the British Isles* (London 1987), no. 183, with colour plate.

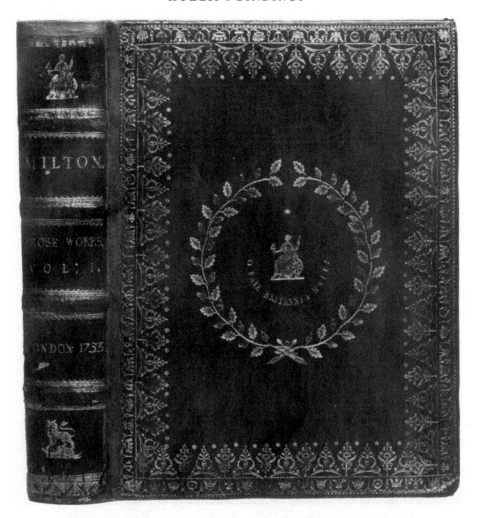

12 Binding by Montagu on vol. 1 of Milton's *Prose Works* (London 1753–56) presented to Harvard College by Thomas Hollis, 1758 (cover excluding spine, 30 × 24.5 cm)

considerable additions by the author. He at once prepared a lengthy cancel dated 1756, also issued as a separate publication with a title-page and explanatory preface. All observed copies of the *Prose Works* in Hollis bindings contain this cancel instead of the original leaves, providing a likely *terminus a quo* for the practice of reinforcing printed propaganda by emblematic binding.

It is not so easy to guess when Hollis stopped employing Montagu, but cumulative evidence suggests that their relationship was fairly

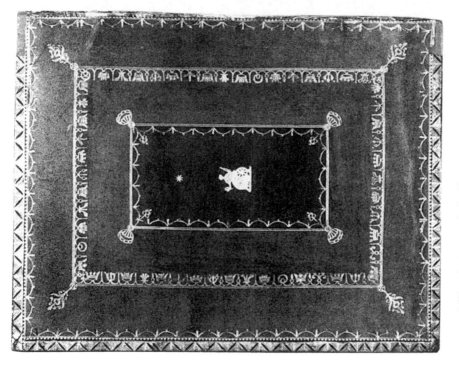

13–14 Milton's *Prose Works* (London 1753–56), vol. I, front (left) and back doublure, bound by Richard Montagu (cover excluding spine, 30 × 24.5 cm)

short. To begin with, Montagu's bindings are very few compared with the wholesale quantities produced by Hollis's later binders. Of more than 300 emblematic bindings that I have personally examined, fewer than twenty are by Montagu; published references and reports indicate the existence of perhaps twenty or thirty more by him, but a much larger number by other hands. Hollis's *Diary* (beginning, as noted, on 14 April 1759) contains no reference to Montagu, although Matthewman and Shove are frequently mentioned by name, and a few other binders occasionally appear. The tone of these references seems to indicate that Matthewman and Shove were already well known to Hollis and executing bindings for him in 1759, and that he had ceased employing Montagu.

CIPRIANI'S DESIGNS

Sometime in 1758 or early 1759 Hollis decided to improve on the limited and rather makeshift stock of emblematic tools used by Montagu. The plan to scatter his liberty texts far and wide – *ut spargam* became one of his favourite mottoes – was growing in his mind. Collaboration with James Stuart on medals celebrating victories in the Seven Years' War and the increasing dominance of Britain in world trade may also have inspired him; the medals incorporated many of the same emblematic elements.[1] He commissioned the design and cutting of an extensive set of tools that would be specifically his, intended not only to call attention to a book but also to convey through emblems his view of its contents. His scheme went so far that certain emblems could (and did) express a negative connotation when inverted.[2]

Giovanni Battista Cipriani (1727–85), whom Hollis had known in Rome and who had emigrated to England in 1755, executed drawings of seventeen carefully chosen emblems.[3] Two were drawn in two versions each: a cock about to crow and one in the act of crowing (numbers 3 and 6), and a harpy with Medusa's head in its talons in

[1] The series of medals began with designs signalling the taking of Louisbourg in 1758, and continued to the end of the war. See Edward Hawkins *Medallic Illustrations of the History of Great Britain and Ireland* (London 1885) 2, nos. 404 ff.; Laurence Brown *A Catalogue of British Historical Medals* ([London 1980]) 1, nos. 6 ff.

[2] For example, on Jean Hardouin *Ad censuram scriptorum veterum prolegomena* (London 1766) (x 27.20.28*), which has the owl (wisdom) inverted six times on boards and spine; it is a Jesuit publication. [3] Harvard, pfMS Typ 576 (15).

49

	1	
	2	
3		5
	4	
6	7	8

15 Giovanni Battista Cipriani's drawings for Hollis's tools: card 1, designs 1–8

9	10	11
12	13	14
15	17	19
16	18	

16 Giovanni Battista Cipriani's drawings for Hollis's tools: card 2, designs 9–19

profile and full face (numbers 5 and 8): a set of nineteen drawings. All were cut as tools except numbers 5 and 6. Liberty (number 4) was cut in two sizes and Britannia (number 13) in two versions, each in two sizes, making a total of twenty-one tools based on seventeen designs.

The drawings are undated, but it is likely that they were completed before the earliest entry in the *Diary*, which contains many entries concerning various stages of the execution of most other commissions given Cipriani, but no mention of the drawings for the tools or their cutting. It seems highly unlikely that Hollis would fail to record the progress of work so central to his interests and activities. Nor does the *Diary* name the craftsman who engraved the original set of tools or discuss his work, although, as we shall see, when a duplicate set of tools had to be cut in 1764 numerous *Diary* entries refer to the project and identify Thomas Pingo and his sons as the engravers. One may conclude that both the drawings and the first set of tools were in existence before mid-April of 1759.

A shift of symbolism may indicate more narrowly when the drawings and the tools were produced. Montagu's Britannia bears an olive branch in the right hand, and so does she in Cipriani's drawing and in what I believe are the two earliest cuttings of his design; they certainly are rarer in occurrence.[1] Somewhat more common are the three Britannias bearing a trident instead. Surely that reflects growing British dominance of the seas in the Seven Years' War, well advanced by 1758 and virtually absolute by 1759. Two medals with which Hollis was involved in 1758 celebrated the capture of Louisbourg and the taking of Goree, both of which bear a head of Britannia in profile, the motto O FAIR BRITANNIA HAIL, and a trident (see plate 17, from a specimen in the present writer's collection). Britannia with a palm branch does not appear on any book known to have been bound after 1759–60.

The completed tools were put into Matthewman's hands. There is no evidence that anyone else used them during the next decade. A Montagu binding on a tract volume at Harvard appears to show when Hollis turned from Montagu to Matthewman and the Cipriani tools. The latest of three pamphlets it contains is Robert Clayton *The Bishop of Clogher's Speech, Made in the House of Lords* (London 1758).[2] The binding bears Montagu's medium and small Britannias and the smaller lion, but one Britannia on the spine is covered by a thin patch of red morocco tooled with the first version of the Cipriani liberty-cap (7a). Matthew-

---

[1] See discussion of this design, no. 13, below.   [2] *EC75.H7267.zz752t.

17 Britannia, obverse of bronze medal designed by James Stuart and
Thomas Hollis to celebrate the British capture of Goree, 1758

man must have been involved in that small change. On the evidence, we
may conclude that Hollis's employment of Montagu probably began in
1756 and ended some time in 1758.

Hollis at once began to have the new tools stamped on bindings for his
own library and to be given away in large numbers, but the period of his
greatest activity did not begin until 1764 when early in March news
reached London of the catastrophic fire that had destroyed the library
of Harvard College, the most considerable library in British North
America, and part of an institution that had been the object of Hollis
family benefactions for more than fifty years. The next day he started to
collect books to rebuild its collection, and to rally others to do the same.

In June 1764, when this good work was well under way, Matthewman's shop burned down, destroying all the tools along with a large
number of books. No lives were lost, but all the contents of the building
perished. Hollis recorded in his *Diary* on 6 June:

Lamented this misfortune on many accounts; but cheered Mathewman all I could.
I have lost by it a large and *very fine* collection of books, relating chiefly to
Government, which were there for binding, and were intended to be sent to
Harvard College in N. E.; besides much *time* and *thinking*. I will not be discouraged,
however, but begin collecting a finer parcel for that College; and I thank God, that
it was not my own house that was consumed; a Calamity that would have mastered
my poor Philosophy!

He immediately set to work to list to the best of his recollection what
books had been lost, and within a week began giving want-lists to
dealers, the first going to Samuel Baker of York Street, Covent Garden,
progenitor of the firm now known as Sotheby's. Other lists followed
shortly, and Hollis also scoured the bookshops of London almost daily to
see what else he could add. The binderies of Matthewman and Shove
can hardly have done much other work while inundated with the spate

of acquisitions for Harvard. Until new tools could be engraved, Hollis had either to extract symbolic bindings from his own library or send books with other decorations.

On 30 July Matthewman's partner, John Bailey, called on Hollis to pay him £27 insurance for the lost books and £5 2s. 6d. for the tools. Early in November Hollis engaged Thomas Pingo (1692–1776), later assistant engraver at the Royal Mint and already a fine craftsman, and his sons Lewis and John, to re-cut the tools after Cipriani's designs. Despite several consultations over the next sixty days, only ten of the tools were cut promptly. The figure of Libertas was the only tool to be re-cut in two sizes (4b1, 4b2), the smaller of which occurs relatively seldom. Based on their frequency of occurrence and their conjunction on bindings and in smoke prints, one may surmise that the first ten tools to be re-cut were 1b, 2b, 3b, 4b1, 7b, 11b, 13c, 14b, 16b, and 19b.

The diary records the first distribution of copies of John Wallis's *Grammatica linguae anglicanae*, probably the earliest books to bear the new emblematic tools, on 22 December 1764. As late as 5 February 1766, Hollis was still urging Pingo to complete the set. It was a month later that the youngest Pingo brought the seven remaining tools, receiving two guineas for them next day. No doubt this long delay accounts for the relative scarcity of occurrence of some of the tools. I have found no examples of a second cutting of 14 (Insect pierced by arrow), 19 (Cornucopia), and 16 (Trident), and it seems highly likely that they were never re-cut.

On 6 March 1766 Shove reported that Matthewman was in grave financial difficulties, apparently through indiscretions of his partner Bailey, but somehow the crisis was surmounted. Matthewman continued in charge of the emblematic tools until 21 June 1769, when for whatever reason his business failed and he absconded to evade debtors' prison. Hollis does not mention him again in the *Diary*.

The tools, however, survived and found their way into Shove's hands, at least for a few years. In the absence of a written record, a shop practice of Shove's is enough to prove the transfer. Whenever he had to centre a design on a cover, his habit was to pierce the approximate location with an awl or needle. These holes, more prominent than the marks left by Montagu's compasses, are clearly visible, though usually not precisely in the middle of the tool or design as stamped (as in the enlarged detail from a binding known to be by Shove, plate 18). Matthewman apparently needed no such guide, and the presence or absence of pricking is a sure means of differentiating the work of the two shops. Shove continued this practice when using the emblematic tools. A book

18   Pricking to locate centre of cover on a binding by John Shove;
enlarged 2 ×

bound shortly before Hollis's death shows Shove's characteristic piercing of the front and back covers and bears an assortment of tools from the second set, stamped in gold on the covers and spine and inside as smoke prints.[1]

After Hollis's death, Brand Hollis continued to have the tools stamped on bindings that he commissioned, but some were evidently lost, worn, or damaged over the years, and he had four of them (1c, 4c, 7d, and 13d) newly cut, following Cipriani's designs. These re-cuttings as well as imitations from other sources will be noted and illustrated in the subsequent discussion of the individual tools. As late as 1802 the Reverend John Disney, who inherited Brand Hollis's library (which incorporated Hollis's), was still using at least one of Brand Hollis's tools, the figure of Liberty (4c). The binding on which it appears, like other bindings for Brand Hollis and for Disney, still exhibits the piercing of the covers characteristic of John Shove.[2] The date of Shove's death is not known, and it is possible that by that time the 'Son' of Shove's trade-card may have been carrying on the business – and the shop practices – of his father, who seems to have commenced work about 1756.

CIPRIANI'S TOOLS AND THEIR IMITATIONS

The introduction of the tools designed by Cipriani brings with it a host of complications, only the first of which is the distinction between the first set of them to be cut and the second, produced after Matthewman's fire of 1764. The rarer tools can be positively identified as belonging to

[1] The Harvard copy of Theophilus Lindsey *A Farewell Address to the Parishioners of Catterick* (London 1774 [i.e. 1773]), (*EC75.H7267.zz773l), annotated by Hollis on the front flyleaf: 'An honest man's the noblest work of God', a quotation from Pope's *Essay on Man*. Not a Hollis gift to Harvard; presented in 1968 by Mrs Lawrence Churchill.

[2] On Erasmus *The Complaint of Peace* tr. Vicesimus Knox (London 1802); copy in the present writer's collection.

either the pre- or post-fire sets through their association on bindings or in smoke prints with previously identified tools. In general, those of the second set are more faithful renditions of Cipriani's drawings and executed with more grace, and all but a few can be distinguished by measurement alone. But, as noted, four were re-cut for Thomas Brand Hollis, and some of Hollis's emblems were copied as binder's tools or in other ways by various of his contemporaries. The institutional libraries to which Hollis sent quantities of books also received gifts of money from him to enrich their collections – Bern by bequest, and Zürich during his lifetime. Bern caused five of Hollis's emblematic tools to be imitated by local craftsmen, and Zürich two, so that their additions could be related visually to the books already sent from England.[1] At least four persons adapted designs for their own use. Several special presentation copies of James Stuart and Nicholas Revett *The Antiquities of Athens* include Hollis symbols in a plaque onlaid on the front cover of Volumes I and II (London 1762–87), and in a corner of an engraved map in Volume II, p. v.[2] Count Francesco Algarotti (another friend and correspondent of Hollis) used still more of the symbols in the engraved frontispiece and title of his *Opere* (Livorno 1764).

The garland of oak leaves around Britannia in Cipriani's drawing was cut as a part of only one large tool. The star that sometimes appears above symbolic tools was added with a small tool, evidently for decorative emphasis. In works by Sir Isaac Newton and a few other favourite writers, their initials were added to the smoke prints.

Most of the emblems derive from Greek or Roman coins, with one or two from other classical antiquities probably from Hollis's own extensive cabinet and collection or from his reference library. The late Miss Emma L. Pafort of the Pierpont Morgan Library worked for many years to identify Hollis's sources and to attempt to assign a significance to each. I have been kindly granted access to her unpublished typescript, 'Symbols on Hollis Bindings' (New York 1950),[3] and am grateful to her for her numismatic work, but it must be stated that she

---

[1] On Hollis's bindings at Bern, see Johann Lindt 'Die Berner Buchbinder Gabriel Freudenberger, Vater und Sohn' *Stultifera navis* 3/4 (1950), pp. 118–25, and Charles Ramsden 'The Collection of Hollis Bindings at Berne' *The Book Collector* 7 (1958), pp. 164–70; both reproduce both genuine and imitation Hollis tools. On the general Hollis collection at Bern, see Hans Bloesch 'Ein Englischer Gönner der Berner Stadtbibliothek im 18. Jahrhundert' *Festschrift Gustav Binz* (Basle 1935), pp. 112–18, and Hans Utz *Die Hollis–Sammlung in Bern* (Bern [1959]), the latter with many details about the nature of the collection. I am not aware of any similar studies of the collection given to Zürich.
[2] See Nixon *Five Centuries*, no. 69.   [3] Pierpont Morgan Library, 831/B89.

19   Appliqué plaque on presentation binding, vol. 1 of James Stuart
and Nicholas Revett, *Antiquities of Athens* (London 1762) (diameter of
plaque, 13.5 cm)

did not fully differentiate the two sets of tools and did not discuss the
contemporary imitations. The present study concentrates on the tools
themselves; it depends to some extent on Miss Pafort for their sources,
but does not always agree on their significance. Dr David Gordon
Mitten, James Loeb Professor of Classical Art and Archaeology at
Harvard University, and Dr Cornelius Vermeule of the Boston
Museum of Fine Arts have kindly examined Cipriani's designs, refining
Miss Pafort's identifications and pointing out specific sources in a
substantial number of cases. I remain, of course, responsible for the
conclusions that I draw.

Close examination reveals numerous differences between the two
cuttings of tools as well as their imitations. The following remarks are
limited to those sufficient to distinguish them. The letter 'a' has been

20   Engraved title and frontispiece of vol. 1 of Francesco Algarotti's
Opere, incorporating emblems also used by Hollis

assigned to tools of the first set, and (except for Britannia, which is
unusually complicated), 'b' to the second set. When possible, smoke
prints are reproduced as well, because they reveal details of cutting
usually somewhat obscured in the gilt tooling. Other versions are
assigned arbitrary letter designations. The numbers are keyed to the
illustrative plates, which are as nearly as possible actual size.

THE TOOLS

1. Seated owl. 1a is 17 mm tall, oval-bodied, and stands directly on a
base with vertical hatching. 1b is 19 mm tall and much closer to the
naturalistic appearance of Cipriani's drawing; it stands on a trapezoidal
base which is in turn on a larger base with vertical hatching. The pupils

| 1a | 1b | 1b
smoke
print | 1c
Brand
Hollis | 1d
Bern | 1e
Zürich |

21   Tools based on design no. 1: seated owl

of its eyes achieve a threatening look by being cut as spirals.[1] Brand Hollis had the tool re-cut (1c); it is 20 mm tall, stands directly on a base with vertical hatching coarser than that of 1a, the wing set off by a bold line and with well-defined wing feathers and eyes made by dark circles surrounding solid round pupils. The Bern imitation (1d) is 19 mm tall and oval-bodied like 1a. Its ears, particularly that to the viewer's right, curve downward. It appears to be standing on a disc.[2] The Zürich imitation (1e) also resembles 1a; its height is 17 mm, and its eyes appear to be looking down and to the left of the viewer, while those of 1a look to the right.[3]

The owl, attribute of Athena, was obviously chosen to symbolize wisdom and learning, but in Cipriani's version it is naturalistic and quite unlike the conventional owls found on Athenian coinage. It is the symbol most often inverted on Hollis bindings to denote disapproval (or the lack of wisdom) of the contents.

2. Owl with wings spread, a palm branch in its talons. (The palm branch has been mistakenly called a quill pen, probably because of the shape of its cut end, but comparison with the acknowledged palm branch, no. 9 below, confirms its identity.) 2a is 21 mm tall, and 2b is 25 mm. 2b can be readily differentiated by the fact that the fifth palm frond from the left curves so that its tip touches the sixth frond.[4]

A similar design is found on the 'new style' tetradrachm of Athens.[5]

[1] *The Rothschild Library* 2, plate 58 and p. 751, illustrates and discusses a selection of the Hollis tools with numbering differing from the present study. 1a = Rothschild 7a, 1b = Rothschild 7b.

[2] I am indebted to Mrs Margaret Eschler for confirming the measurements of the tools on bindings at Bern. A rubbing of 1d is illustrated by Lindt (see above, note 1 p. 56), p. 119 no. 5.

[3] Herr Ludwig Kohler kindly supplied excellent photocopies of the two imitation tools found on books at Zürich.   [4] 2a = Rothschild 8.

[5] Information from Professor David Gordon Mitten, who also provided identifications and other essential information for designs nos. 7, 13, 14, 15, and 16.

2a   2b   2b
                                                                       smoke print

22   Tools based on design no. 2: owl and palm branch

To Hollis it seems to have signified the victory of wisdom in the cause of peace. His diary records that on 30 July 1759 he gave to the British Museum a unique medal with a bust of Milton on the obverse, and this symbol on the reverse with the legend BY DEEDS OF PEACE, another of his favourite mottoes and a quotation from *Paradise Regained*. The medal was undoubtedly struck on Hollis's commission. He also had a signet ring made with a stone of chalcedony engraved with the same emblem and motto.

One notable binding given to Harvard fully exploits its emblematic possibilities. The volume, in red morocco, contains two Massachusetts election sermons by Andrew Eliot and Jonathan Mayhew, the earlier deploring passage of the Stamp Act, the other celebrating its repeal. The spine bears four imprints of the seated owl (1b). The back cover begins a motto derived from Sallust *Bellum Iugurthinum* x.6, 'DISCORDIA RES MAXIMAE DILABVNTVR'; the front cover concludes it, 'CONCORDIA RES PARVAE CRESCVNT'. Above the first part of the motto is the short sword (14b) point downward, signifying conflict; below it, the owl and palm inverted, signifying the end of peaceful pursuits. On the other cover the owl and palm are in normal position over the motto, and the sword is point upward (inverted) below. The intended symbolism could hardly be clearer.[1]

3. Cock with beak closed. Both versions are 21 mm tall. The feet of 3b are firmly planted in its base, but in 3a they are on top of the base. 3b has prominent spurs, but they are hardly noticeable in 3a. 3c is the imitation cut in Bern, and is 24 mm tall. It is easily identified as the only version with tufts of grass at the bird's feet.[2]

The cock is found on Greek coins of Himera in Sicily, and Hollis may have taken it as a symbol of freedom or enlightenment; some have

[1] On the cameo cut by Natter for the ring, see *Memoirs*, pp. 799, 839. The emblematic binding is Harvard *AC75.E1441.765sba.   [2] 3c = Lindt 4.

60

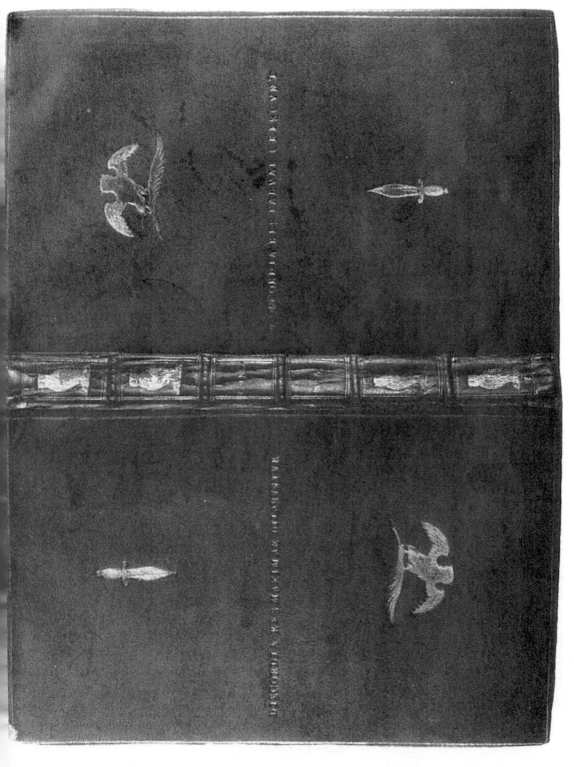

23 Binding on Stamp Act sermons of Jonathan Mayhew and Andrew Eliot (front cover size, 20.4 × 13 cm)

3a   3b   3b   3c
                                     smoke print   Bern

24   Tools based on design no. 3: cock

thought it may signify vigilance and watchfulness. It is also associated with Aesculapius (see tool no. 16, below). The cock of Gaul and the cock of Portugal may have a similar derivation, but it is unlikely that Hollis had either of them in mind.

4. Liberty (Libertas). 4a occurs in two sizes: 4a1, 31 mm tall, and 4a2, 21 mm tall. In both the figure stands on a small base on top of a larger one, the latter apparently the engraver's interpretation of the ground and shadow in Cipriani's drawing. 4b also occurs in two sizes, in both of which she stands on a small base without further underpinning. 4b1 is 38 mm tall, 4b2 is 29 mm tall. Another version of the tool was cut for Thomas Brand Hollis (4c), 37 mm tall. It can be distinguished from the others by the liberty-pole, distinctly shorter than the figure, and the greater detail of its clothing.[1]

Libertas was a goddess of the Roman republic found in both coinage and sculpture, and naturally of great interest to Hollis. She is associated with the pileus (see no. 7, below), which she always holds in her right hand. Hollis sent £20 to an Italian friend, the antiquary Abbate Ridolfino Venuti (1705–63), to assist in compiling and publishing his monograph, *De dea libertate* (Rome 1763), sheets of which did not reach Hollis in England until after the author's death. The plates in Venuti's book represent many of the coins that provided sources for this and other symbols earlier adopted by Hollis.

5. Harpy clutching a severed head, profile. Not cut.

6. Cock crowing. Not cut.

7. Liberty-cap (pileus), the distinctive fur cap granted to Roman freedmen. This was Hollis's favourite symbol; it occurs in most of his liberty-prints, and he even had a typographical version made, which

---

[1]   4a2 = Rothschild 1.

4a1

4a1
smoke
print

4a2

4b1

4b1
smoke
print

4b2

4c
Brand
Hollis

25   Tools based on design no. 4: Liberty

appears on title-pages and elsewhere in some of the books that he caused
to be published. 7a is 15 mm tall, and the fur is represented by rather stiff
shading in a chevron-like pattern; 7b is 12 mm tall, with much more
realistic fur and some diagonal shading on the lower left side.[1] 7c is the
typographical version, 7 mm tall. 7d is a re-cutting for Brand Hollis, 12
mm tall. It lacks the diagonal shading found on the lower left of 7b and
the fur appears to be in more pronounced tufts. 7e is a version, 8 mm tall,
used by (and presumably cut for) Joseph Gulston (1745–86). It is found
at an angle in the four corners of the covers of a russia binding on
Gulston's extra-illustrated copy of Francis Peck *Memoirs of the Life &
Actions of Oliver Cromwell* (London 1740) in the Houghton Library. 7f, g,
and h are narrowly different versions found on a number of calf bindings
on the third edition of James Boswell *Account of Corsica* (London 1769) –

---

[1] 7b = Rothschild 2.

63

| 7a | 7a
smoke
print | 7b | 7c
typographic | 7d
Brand
Hollis |

| 7e
Gulston | 7f
Boswell | 7g
Boswell | 7h
Boswell |

26   Tools based on design no. 7: liberty-cap

two copies, displaying between them all three variants of this imitation, in the Houghton Library – and on copies of his *Essays in Favour of the Brave Corsicans* (London 1769) in the Beinecke Library at Yale and the Rothschild collection at Cambridge.[1] They are respectively 12 mm, 11 mm, and 10 mm tall. Their horizontal shading distinguishes them from all other versions of the cap. It is puzzling that the binder should have had three tools so close in design and differing so little in size.

The pileus was the cap originally associated with the Dioscuri, Castor and Pollux, the heavenly twins, who were believed to have taken the field at the decisive battle of Lake Regillus in 496 BC. Before its use by the Romans, it appeared on a variety of Greek coins, usually in pairs, and on some of them it had a narrow brim as in Hollis's tool no. 13a2, below. It was treated at length by Venuti in *De dea libertate*. It is quite distinct from the Phrygian cap that later became a symbol of revolution in France and that is sometimes found on French bindings of that period.

The pileus not only symbolized freedom, it represented the right of citizens to take up arms in defence of their rights. It appears flanked by two short swords on the denarius of Marcus Brutus celebrating the Ides

---

[1] I am indebted to Miss Marjorie Wynne and Dr David McKitterick for information about the Yale (Beinecke) and Rothschild examples.

64

8a   8a   8b
smoke
print

27   Tools based on design no. 8: harpy with severed head

of March[1] (see no. 14, below), which is one of the coins depicted in
Venuti's book. The same triple symbol appears on a number of Hollis
bindings, on the socle of the heroic marble bust of Hollis by Joseph
Wilton, and on the base of the bust of Hollis in the engraving by Cipriani
that is the usual frontispiece to Blackburne's *Memoirs*.

Hollis's own copy (now in the Houghton Library) of Thomas Fuller
Sovereigns Prerogative and the Subjects Priviledge (London 1657), which deals
with political events during 3 and 4 Charles I, is bound in polished
sprinkled calf with the pileus (1a) in the centre of the front cover
surrounded by an array of four swords (14a) and four clubs of Hercules
(17a), a style of design that I have seen elsewhere only in smoke prints,
although not with this combination of tools.[2] Such combinations must
signify the right of free men to use force in overthrowing tyranny.

8. Harpy clutching a severed head (actually the head of Medusa), full
face. This design has been miscalled, on the basis of its gilt impression, a
sphinx, or a chimera holding a mask; but Cipriani's drawing for the
unused profile version (no. 5 above) confirms the present nomenclature.
8a is 27 mm tall, 8b 21 mm.[3] Examples of 8b are rare: it was probably
one of the tools delayed in the re-cutting.

Dr Cornelius Vermeule has pointed out that this design is found on
Italo-Etruscan intaglio gems of the first century BC.[4] Medusa's head also
commonly appears on the shield of Athena, as it is shown (for example)
in the engraving often used on late seventeenth-century publications of

[1] A specimen of the coin is in the Frederick M. Watkins Collection of the Fogg Art Museum,
Harvard University.
[2] For the bust and the engraving, see plates 3 and 4. The binding is Harvard
*EC65.F9594.654gaa.
[3] 8b = Rothschild 9.   [4] In correspondence with the author.

28   Array of smoke prints preceding *Duc de Belle-Isle Lettres* ([n.p.] 1759)

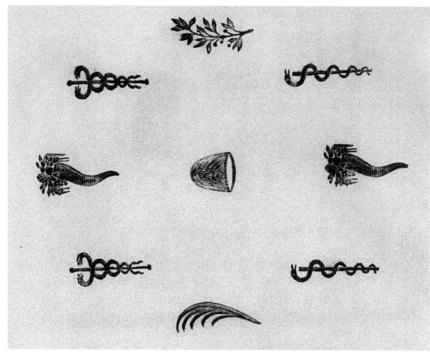

29   Array of smoke prints preceding *Proceedings of the Committee . . . for Cloathing French Prisoners of War* (London 1760)

the Oxford University Press. This depicts Athena seated before the Sheldonian Theatre; she holds a staff in the manner of Libertas and Britannia, and beside her lies another shield bearing the caduceus of Mercury. A contemporary medal struck to commemorate the death of Charles I bears in the centre of its obverse the head of Medusa above a flaming sword, point upwards. Hollis, connoisseur and collector of coins and medals, was surely aware of this one, and would find it an apt symbol for the overthrow of tyranny, with particular reference to Charles I.

In one of his more elaborate smoke-printed designs, 8a is stamped in the middle of an oval composed of eight impressions of the short sword (14b). This display precedes an edition of the Duc de Belle-Isle's *Lettres* ([n.p.] 1759), which Hollis often had bound before the *Proceedings of the Committee. . . for Cloathing French Prisoners of War* (London 1760), to contrast the French commander's callous attitude towards his enemies and his own troops with the humanity demonstrated by the British. The *Report* itself is preceded by a leaf of smoke prints of emblems denoting peace and prosperity. The Harvard copy of [Jean de Serres] *An Historical Collection of the Most Memorable Accidents, and Tragicall Massacres of France* (London 1598; STC 11275), recounting atrocities mainly perpetrated against Protestants, bears on its spine two harpies (8a), two swords (14a), and one club (17a). Brand Hollis evidently appreciated its significance: on the spine of a copy of the duodecimo edition of Blackburne's defence of Milton given to Harvard in 1780, 8b appears twice along with two impressions of the lyre (10b), in allusion to Milton's dual involvement with politics and poetry.[1]

9. Palm branch. Both 9a and 9b are 27 mm tall, but they are readily differentiated because 9b is much more gracefully cut. The ends of the fronds in 9a form a more or less straight line; in 9b they form a curve.[2] The design has sometimes been mistaken for a quill pen.

Again Miss Pafort suggests no immediate numismatic source, but at least from classical times the palm branch has been a standard attribute of figures of Victory. Cipriani's engraving 'O·FAIR·BRITANNIA· HAIL' (1760), most conveniently found as one of the frontispieces to Blackburne's *Memoirs*, depicts on each shoulder of Britannia a small Victory flourishing a palm; 'Britannia Victrix' engraved by Cipriani in

---

[1] On the medal commemorating Charles I, see Christopher Eimer *British Commemorative Medals and Their Values* (London 1987) p. 43 no. 161. Belle-Isle, Harvard *EC75.H7267.zz759b (B)*; Jean de Serres, Harvard STC 11275; Blackburne, Harvard 14495.8*. [2] 9a = Rothschild 13.

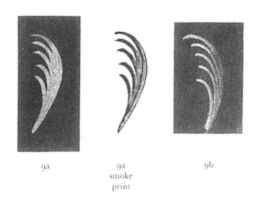

9a   9a   9b
smoke
print

30   Tools based on design no. 9: palm branch

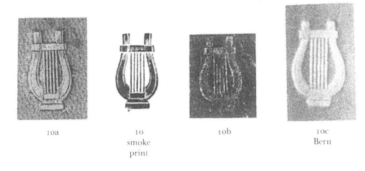

10a   10   10b   10c
smoke   Bern
print

31   Tools based on design no. 10: lyre

1770 after a cameo cut for Hollis by Lorenz Natter in 1754, shows a large Victory with a palm in the left hand, while her right holds a laurel wreath over Britannia's head (*Memoirs*, facing p. 824).

10. Lyre. Both 10a and 10b are 20 mm tall; 10a has a single line running down the inner and outer edges of the curved sides of the body, while 10b has multiple lines of shading following the curves. 10c, the Bern imitation, is 22 mm tall and its curved sides are solidly shaded.[1]

The lyre is a common motif on Greek and Roman coins, symbol of Apollo and Orpheus and hence of music and literature, particularly poetry. Hollis's interest in *belles-lettres* was limited to a relatively small range of poets – Shakespeare, Milton, Marvell, Pope, Glover, and Akenside, for example, not all of whose works he caused to be bound – so the lyre is not often found on his bindings. On the back cover of volume 2 of Baron's edition of Milton in the Niedersächsische Staats- und Universitätsbibliothek Göttingen (see below, no. 13), 10a is twice

---

[1] 10b = Rothschild 11; 10c = Lindt 6.

68

11a   11a smoke print   11b   11b smoke print

32   Tools based on design no. 11: olive branch

12a

33   Tool based on design no. 12: insect and arrow

stamped inverted, flanking the harpy (8a). Here the reference to the execution of Charles I and Milton's diversion from poetry to politics and prose seems abundantly clear.

11. Olive branch. 11a is 27 mm tall, 11b 28 mm. 11b is much more gracefully cut and more faithful to Cipriani's drawing, and the cut end of the branch terminates in a sharp point, while 11a is blunt.[1]

Miss Pafort identifies this symbol as a laurel branch, but the drawing seems quite specifically to represent the olive, confirmed by its clear delineation and the manner of its use in several liberty-prints, as well as in the medals and some of the tools depicting Britannia. It is a common motif in classical coins. It stands, of course, for peace.

12. Insect, or butterfly, and arrow. This is one of the rarest tools; I have seen 12a on a single book at Harvard, [Filippo Buonarroti] *Osservazioni sopra alcuni frammenti di vasi antichi di vetro* (Florence 1716). It also occurs on eight volumes in the Stadt- und Universitätsbibliothek

---

[1]   11b = Rothschild 12.

Bern. It is 27 mm tall. I have yet to see an example of 12b, if indeed it was ever cut.[1]

The emblem derives from both Greek and Roman vase paintings and intaglios, and stands for the human soul. As such it dates from about the fifth century BC, when it was sometimes alternatively pictured as a female figure. Plate XXVIII of Buonarroti's book, taken from a Roman vase, combines both conceptions: a female figure with smooth wings shaped and spotted like those in Cipriani's design is embraced by Cupid, whose wings are feathered. A long passage in the text, pp. 196–7, explores at length the anthropomorphic Psyche and her symbolism as Anima, the soul or spirit. An additional link between this symbol and Hollis is provided by a medal recorded as being in his cabinet. It is illustrated in an engraving by Francesco Bartolozzi in Blackburne's *Memoirs* opposite p. 586 and described in the Appendix, p. 833: a memorial to Francis Hutcheson (1694–1746), the Scottish philosopher, commissioned by Basil Hamilton, Earl of Selkirk. The dies were cut by Antonio Selvi of Florence after a portrait in wax by Isaac Gosset the elder. The obverse represents a bust of Hutcheson; the reverse, a female mourner seated on a funerary urn or tomb and leaning on two closed books, while to her left a butterfly takes flight, symbolizing the ascent of Hutcheson's soul or spirit.

The arrow symbolizes the tortures inflicted on Psyche by Cupid (or Eros) in some versions of the myth. Precisely how Hollis intended the tool remains obscure. Obviously he did not find it widely useful.

13. Britannia. Counting imitations, I have recorded nine contemporary varieties of this tool. Cipriani's drawing shows Britannia seated on a globe, an olive branch in her right hand, a staff with liberty-cap in her left, and a British shield leaning against her, the whole within an oval wreath of oak leaves. Copies of Baron's edition of Milton's *Prose Works* presented to Göttingen in 1761 and Stockholm in 1762 have a faithful rendition (13a1) of Cipriani's design stamped on the front cover; the wreath is 67 mm tall and the figure within is 37 mm. The tool is so large

---

[1] Harvard Typ 725.16.246* (B); the other volumes bearing this tool in the Stadt- und Universitätsbibliothek Bern are Walter Moyle *The Works* 3 vols. (London 1726–27) (Hollis 140); Thomas Burnet *De statu mortuorum et resurgentium tractatus* (London 1733) (Hollis 198); Francis Hutcheson *An Essay on the nature and Conduct of the Passions and Affections* 3rd ed. (London 1742) (Hollis 200) and his *An Inquiry into the Original of Our Ideas of Beauty and Virtue* (London 1725) (Hollis 205); and Michael Geddes *The Church-History of Ethiopia* (London 1696) (Hollis 223). Photocopies of all these bindings have been kindly provided by Mrs Margaret Eschler.

34   Cupid and Psyche, detail from Plate XXVIII of [Filippo Buonarroti] *Osservazioni sopra alcuni frammenti . . .* (Florence 1716) presented to Harvard by Hollis

that it was probably cut as a plaque to be stamped by an arming-press; all the other tools under discussion could be the normal variety on wooden handles, stamped by hand in the usual manner. Curiously enough, one of Hollis's elaborate arrangements of smoke prints in both these copies depicts a different large Britannia (13b1) surrounded by eight tridents (18a).[1] 13a2 is found on a single volume at Harvard, the *Works* of Andrew Marvell (London 1726) which also bears the lyre (10a). It is 19 mm tall, and the liberty-cap may be improvized with a separate small tool; it has a brim not otherwise found in Hollis tools or engravings, though sometimes found on classical coins.[2] Then, as noted earlier, Hollis decided to replace the olive branch with a trident. 13b1 is 37 mm tall and 13b2 21 mm; the tridents held by both are barbed. The globes on which all four of the preceding are seated are solidly shaded with concentric circles. 13c, the post-fire version, is 37 mm tall, and easily recognized because the trident lacks barbs and the globe is a simple outline without shading. All of these face left. 13d is a re-cutting for Brand Hollis, readily differentiated by the rounded prongs on the trident as well as other less obvious differences. 13e, the Bern imitation,

[1]   Photocopies, rubbings, and other information about these copies were kindly supplied by Dr Reimer Eck and Dr Mirjam M. Foot. The Göttingen and Stockholm bindings are not identical in every detail.

[2]   The pileus with a brim can be seen on a Carthaginian coin in the collection of the Museum of Fine Arts, Boston, Massachusetts.

13a1

13a2

13b1

13b1
smoke
print

13b2

13c

13c
smoke
print

13d
Brand
Hollis

13e
Bern

13f
Hanway

13g
Hawkesworth

35   Tools based on design no. 13: Britannia

14a   14   14b   14c
      smoke   Zürich
      print

36   Tools based on design no. 14: short sword

faces right, has a barbed trident, and is 22 mm tall. 13f, a version
apparently cut for Jonas Hanway, faces left, has a palm branch in the
right hand, and a barbed trident in the left; it is 24 mm tall. On some
bindings Hanway employed a small head of Britannia in profile
encircled with the motto borrowed from Hollis, 'O fair Britannia hail',
but he does not appear to have used the motto with the seated figure. 13f
was used by John Hawkesworth on a presentation binding on a copy of
his *Adventures of Telemachus* (London 1768). It faces left, is 21 mm tall,
holds an olive branch in the right hand, and lacks a liberty-cap; unlike
all the others, but like Montagu's Britannias, the lower edge of the shield
is above ground level.[1]

It is common knowledge that the figure of Britannia was introduced
by Charles II, modelled upon his mistress the Duchess of Richmond and
Lennox ('La belle Stuart'). Thereafter Britannia appeared in many
versions in pictures and on coins and medals as a symbol of Great
Britain. The farthings and halfpennies of George II and George III
depict her holding an olive branch.

14. Roman short sword or dagger (pugio). 14a is 28 mm tall, its blade
having parallel edges. 14b is 30 mm tall with a leaf-shaped blade.[2] 14c,
the Zürich imitation, is also 30 mm tall with very slightly curved edges,
but it lacks the delicate shading and the prominent central rib of 14b.

The Roman source for the sword is already noted in discussing the
pileus (no. 7). Brutus adopted it from the history of his legendary

---

[1] 13b2 = Rothschild 4; 13e = Lindt 3. 13f is reproduced from Hobson *English Bindings*, p. 120
no. 88 and facing plate; the binding is dated 1763. 13g is reproduced from a photograph
kindly supplied by Mr Patrick King; the binding on which it appears is illustrated and
described in Catalogue 13 of Patrick King Ltd, pp. 14–15 no. 19.

[2] 14b = Rothschild 3.

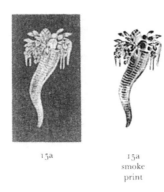

15a

15a
smoke
print

37 Tools based on design no. 15: cornucopia

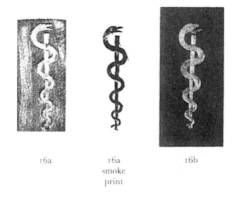

16a

16a
smoke
print

16b

38 Tools based on design no. 16: wand 'of Aesculapius

ancestor, Lucius Junius Brutus, allegedly the founder and first consul of the Roman republic, who in 509 BC was said to have sworn on a bloody dagger to expel the Tarquin kings from Rome.[1] It surely stands for the right to take arms against tyranny or the threat of invasion; Hollis also seems to have employed it to stand for other violent actions. For example, the Bern copy of Michael Geddes *The History of the Churches of Malabar* (London 1694) (Hollis 224), which contains an account of Roman Catholic persecutions of indigenous Christians, bears the sword (14a) on the front cover and the club (17a) on the back. Classical coins, Cipriani's drawing, and Hollis's usage all show that its normal position is vertical with the point down.

[1] On the legendary nature of Lucius Junius Brutus, see Sir Ronald Syme *The Roman Revolution* (Oxford 1939), pp. 59, 85 and notes. Historicity, however, is irrelevant in matters of symbolism. Not many years after Hollis's death, American patriotic orators routinely referred to George Washington as 'the Lucius Junius Brutus of his race'.

74

17a   17b

39   Tools based on design no. 17: club of Hercules

15. Cornucopia. 15a is 27 mm long. I have seen it gilt on a single volume at Bern, *Monumenta vetustatis Kempiana* (London 1720) (Hollis 119), but otherwise only as a smoke print associated with other tools of the first cutting. I have not seen an example of 15b.

The cornucopia is a common motif in classical coinage, especially on coins of the Ptolemies, and it signifies abundance, good fortune, and happiness. The figure of Libertas often holds a cornucopia, and is so seen in Cipriani's engraving of Britannia, cited above.[1]

16. Wand of Aesculapius. 16a is 28 mm tall and its single snake has no tongue; 16b is 30 mm tall with a prominent tongue.[2]

This has many classical representations on coins and elsewhere; for example, on the Hellenistic coins of Pergamon. Its connection with medicine is obvious, but Hollis may also have intended it to symbolize learning in the service of mankind.

17. Club of Hercules. Both versions are 26 mm tall, but 17b is closer to the spirit of Cipriani's drawing, with much more prominent knots visible along the edge.

Miss Pafort traces this design to coins of Commodus and Trajan; it is, of course, a Greek motif as well. On 31 May 1759, without much doubt some time after the tools were first cut, Hollis records acquiring an antique paste of Hercules killing the Hydra with such a club. At the time of the Glorious Revolution, Hercules sometimes served as a symbol for William of Orange. The meaning of the club appears to be power and courage in the defence of freedom, with an added reference to William III and the Protestant establishment. The normal position of the club is vertical, hand-grip uppermost.

[1] See Frank H. Sommer III 'Thomas Hollis and the Arts of Dissent' *Prints in and of America to 1850* ed. John D. Morse (Charlottesville [1970]), p. 143 and figs. 11 and 12.
[2] 16a = Rothschild 6.

75

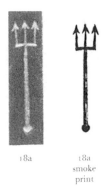

18a   18a
               smoke
               print

40   Tools based on design no. 18: trident

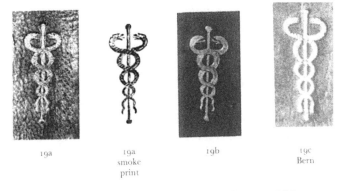

19a   19a   19b   19c
             smoke   Bern
             print

41   Tools based on design no. 19: caduceus of Mercury

18. Trident of Neptune. 18a is 28 mm tall. I have found it gilt on the spine of a single volume given to Bern, Richard Glover *London: or the Progress of Commerce*, 2nd edition (London 1739).[1] It also occurs as a repeated smoke print surrounding a Britannia (13b1) in the sets of Milton given to Göttingen and Stockholm in 1761–62. I have found no example of 18b.

Again this is a common classical motif, and represents domination of the sea.

19. Caduceus of Hermes or Mercury. Both versions are 27 mm tall, but the top coil of the serpents in 19a is 10 mm wide, in 19b 12 mm wide. In 19b the head of the serpent on the right displays a prominent tongue; the tongue is much smaller in 19a. 19c, the Bern imitation, is 29 mm tall and lacks the detailed shading found in 19a and 19b.[2]

[1] Stadt- und Universitätsbibliothek Bern, Hollis 74a.
[2] 19a = Rothschild 5; 19c = Lindt 2.

76

This is another common classical motif. Among other attributes of Hermes, he was the god of commerce, and it seems likely that to Hollis the caduceus symbolized trade and prosperity. A figure of Hermes bearing the caduceus still ornaments the façade of the Royal Society of Arts.

3

Patron and designer

THOMAS HOLLIS'S ENGAGEMENT with the fine arts and the practical arts was intense and complex both in degree and in motivation. At one level he approached the arts as a propagandist, using them to foster the spread and protection of his Whig ideals of civil and religious freedom; at another, as a sympathetic and generous patron of artists and craftsmen, forwarding both the aesthetic and commercial progress of his nation; at a third, as student, connoisseur, collector, and adviser to both artists and fellow-collectors; and at yet another, as a designer of professional ability to whom others could, and did, turn for assistance in dealing with practical and artistic problems. In this capacity, he must be given credit for at least a small part in the development of the neo-classical style in England.

By 1753, when he returned to London from his second Grand Tour of Europe, he had studied at first hand many of the great works of art and antiquity that were then accessible, he had formed a sound and mature taste, he had begun amassing a useful reference library on such subjects and was giving material aid to scholars for the publication of similar works, and he had wide acquaintance with artists and craftsmen of every kind, to say nothing of dealers, antiquarians, and fellow connoisseurs. He had observed archaeological investigations in progress at Pompeii, Herculaneum, Paestum, and other sites, and had viewed objects discovered there in museums and private collections. He seems to have had correspondents everywhere his travels had taken him. Although still in his early thirties, he was already an authority with both knowledge and a keen eye, as his contemporaries soon discovered. For his part he actively enlarged his circle both of friendship and of patronage. His rôle as patron is not widely known, for in this as in other aspects of his personal life he jealously guarded his privacy.

His artistic and antiquarian interests were wide ranging. His home in Pall Mall at the corner of John Street,[1] which he maintained from 1761

[1] John Street is the easterly of the two short streets running between St James's Square and

78

to the end of his life, must have been a smaller version of Sir John Soane's in Lincoln's Inn Fields, which fortunately still provides us with a specimen of a virtuoso's personal collection: a house crammed with paintings, drawings, prints, and sculpture; classical artifacts; and a library – a natural and necessary background for his many activities, and totally unlike the antiseptically scientific galleries of today. Before his fortieth year he was elected to the two most prestigious organizations in London: he became FRS on 30 June 1757, and FSA on 22 December of the same year. Along with his years of residence in Lincoln's Inn, these were the public honours he chose most often to recall in inscriptions and on book-plates. He seems to have attended meetings whenever possible, and to have taken an active, if subordinate, part in their affairs. His resolution to avoid office held firm in these societies as elsewhere, but he willingly served on committees, and through them he inevitably met the intellectual élite of his time.

Even more to the point was his slightly earlier membership in the SPAC, now better known as the Royal Society of Arts, founded in 1754. Its official historians have remarked that the distinction of its members was so great 'that it might almost seem easier to compile a list of the eminent men of the mid-eighteenth century who were *not* members'.[1] Hollis was elected on 17 March 1756, having been proposed by Thomas Major, the engraver. He compounded for life membership in 1759.

Professor John Lawrence Abbott has investigated Hollis's part in the affairs of the Society in considerable detail, using the Society's own records in conjunction with the *Diary*.[2] Abbott tells us of Hollis's participation in numerous committees and in its general meetings, where he was sometimes successful in carrying his ideas in opposition to

Pall Mall. It is no longer dignified by a street sign, and is not identified by name on most modern maps. Hollis's first lodging after returning from his European journeys was in the house of a Mrs Mott in Bedford Street, Covent Garden; but he became convinced that his landlady was mad, and was much relieved when a fire on the premises (*London Chronicle* 22–4 January 1761) provided an excuse to move to more suitable quarters.

[1] Derek Hudson and Kenneth W. Luckhurst *The Royal Society of Arts, 1754–1954* (London 1954), p. 28.

[2] 'Thomas Hollis and the Society 1756–1774' *Journal of the Royal Society of Arts* 119 (1972), pp. 711–15, 803–7, 874–8. The MS. Minutes of the Society, preserved in its library, record Hollis's appointment to a wide variety of committees; the Minutes of Committees record his participation in still more. The discrepancy arises because, in the early days of the Society, any member could participate in any committee, whether or not he had been appointed to it.

those of its officers. He was also active in promoting candidates for membership.[1]

Through the Society Hollis certainly knew and worked with Sir Joshua Reynolds, who served with him on several committees, notably that formed in January 1759 to judge drawings submitted in competition. Hollis was in the chair for its repeated deliberations and reported to the Society as a whole on 14 February (one of the few times he accepted a Chairmanship). For him to chair such a committee with such a member, one must conclude that his artistic judgement was known and respected.[2] Later he took part in the committee that initiated the Society's first art exhibition, an annual affair that soon generated so much controversy among its participants and patrons that a dissident faction formed the Society of Artists with a rival exhibition, while yet another dispute resulted in the formation of the Royal Academy a few years later.

Hollis, whose tastes were, if anything, classical, found little to admire in any of these exhibitions; yet he was certainly interested in contemporary artists. He visited Reynolds's studio at least once, to view the portrait of David Garrick (whom he also knew) between Comedy and Tragedy.[3] And he recorded visits to Hogarth's studio on more than one occasion, subscribing to at least one of Hogarth's prints and receiving a copy of 'The Medley' as a gift from the artist.[4]

Other artists were well known to Hollis and often patronized by him. He commissioned Isaac Gosset to model wax portraits of British heroes of the Commonwealth to present to the University of Leiden. Joseph Wilton, whose marble bust of Hollis we have seen, sometimes consulted

---

[1] In my Sandars Lecture I wrongly stated that Hollis nominated Samuel Johnson for membership; but it was James Stuart who nominated Dr Johnson, and Hollis's nominee was Robert Johnson of Cavenham Hall, Suffolk. See above, note 2 p. 2, and John L. Abbott 'Dr. Johnson and the Society' *Journal of the Royal Society of Arts* 115 (1968), pp. 395–400, 486–91. Between 1757 and 1763 Hollis nominated, or joined in nominating, some thirty candidates for membership. Until 4 May 1763, proposal by a single member sufficed for nomination; after that date, three proposers were required, and Hollis is recorded as joining in only three such nominations.

[2] The committee included, among other more or less eminent graphic artists, Sir Henry Cheere, Allan Ramsay the painter, Thomas Major, James Macardell, Sir William Stuart, James Basire, Joseph Wilton, Joseph Nollekens, Richard Cosway, and Giovanni Battista Cipriani. Another committee chaired by Hollis was charged with preparing the Society's first premium medal, awarded initially in a special version to James Stuart, as a reward for his work on its design. In 1760 Hollis declined to chair the larger Committee on the Polite Arts, which was overseer of all of the Society's activities in literature and the fine arts.

[3] *Diary* 29 August 1761.   [4] *Diary* 28, 30 April 1761; 15 March, 2 April 1762.

him on matters of design, and was eventually commissioned by Hollis among others to execute a heroic statue of Pitt the elder to be erected in Charleston, South Carolina,[1] where it remains to this day. Joseph Nollekens sought Hollis's advice on a bas-relief he planned to submit for the Society's premium,[2] although John Thomas Smith did not find it worth his while to mention the circumstance in his celebrated book of gossip, *Nollekens and His Times* (London 1828). I have mentioned the six Canalettos painted in England to order for Hollis, probably as the result of an introduction from their mutual friend, Consul Joseph Smith (it is possible but unlikely that Hollis met the artist during his Italian sojourn); Smith also introduced another of his protégés, Francesco Zuccarelli, whose work came to grace the walls of the house in Pall Mall. Another of Hollis's commissions was a series of at least four oils, several of them familiar Dorset landscapes, by Pieter Andreas Rysbraeck.[3] And so it goes, through a long line of painters, sculptors, engravers, artists in mezzotint, and specialists in letter-cutting.[4] The identity of some and their relations with Hollis remain to be discovered, and are beyond the scope of this chapter. What is pertinent is the evidence of long, close, and sympathetic contact with a wide spectrum of the artistic world. Hollis was no uncritical enthusiast, as the acerbic comments in his diary on the exhibitions and artifacts fully attest. Thus, when Gustavus Brander insisted on showing him his most prized possession, the ornamented steel chair on which the first Emperor of Germany was said to have been crowned, Hollis was polite but later confided to his *Diary*, 'It is that kind of Curiosity that a good Eye likes to see, but doth not wish to purchase.'

An important link between the artistic community and the bibliographical part of Hollis's activities lay in the small group dominated by Cipriani and including Francesco Bartolozzi, James Basire, and James Macardell, who designed and executed the liberty-prints that formed such an important part of the great Plan for promoting civil and religious freedom. His protégés also included Lorenz Natter, who engraved onyx cameos of liberty subjects for him. Hollis spent much time and did not spare his purse in securing stones with precisely the right colours and stratifications for this purpose. The most important was the *Britannia victrix* executed to precise specifications in 1754,

[1] *Diary* 4 March 1762. [2] *Diary* 17 July 1761.
[3] 'A large picture of Game', *Diary* 9 May 1760; and three Dorset landscapes, including one of Urles Farm, sold at Sotheby, 8 March 1950, lots 129–31.
[4] On virtually all prints commissioned by Hollis, another hand than the artist's cut the inscriptional lettering.

possibly Hollis's first attempt to give graphic expression to his political ideas. Political developments during the next ten or twelve years turned this into an excellent subject for a liberty-print, and in 1769 Cipriani made a free sketch of the *Britannia victrix* which he developed into an etching in the next year.[1] Its quotation concerning Algernon Sidney and the prominent display of the date of the execution of Charles I underline some of the points Hollis wished to make.

Also important is John Baptist Jackson's chiaroscuro woodcut of Algernon Sidney. Hollis discovered that this able artist had fallen on hard times, and partly to benefit him commissioned in 1754 an imposing portrait of a size suitable for insertion in the 1751 folio edition of Sidney's *Discourses Concerning Government*. Jackson's print was based on a drawing by George Vertue which was in turn based on an oil by Justus ab Egmont. The copy of this book sent to Harvard contains a suite of six proofs in varying colours of the four blocks required by the medium; the words below it were cut on a separate block, a proof of which is to be found in Hollis's collection of drawings and proofs.[2] These words were to recur on a print of Sidney by Cipriani in 1760 and in Hollis's unsigned introduction to his own edition of the *Discourses* in 1763. Later we shall meet the same words in revolutionary Massachusetts and, indeed, in present-day Massachusetts.

This is not the place to discuss at length the liberty-prints, except for some intended primarily to illustrate books, but even a partial list of the subjects reflects the roster of Hollis's canonical texts.[3] Among others may be mentioned five portraits of John Milton at different ages, including the satirical 'Milton Victorious over Salmasius', Edmund Ludlow, Andrew Marvell, John Locke, Dr John Wallis, Sir Isaac Newton, Hubert Languet, Bulstrode Whitelocke, Jonathan Mayhew in a memorial print satirizing Archbishop Secker, and Hollis's favourite Whig historian, Catherine Sawbridge Macaulay (later Graham). Nearly every one of these prints contains one or more of the emblems employed on bindings, sometimes slightly modified and not always conspicuously placed: for example, a small owl peeps out of the foliage in many of them. Notes accompanying the drawings and proofs in the

[1] See the article by Sommer (cited above, note 1 p. 75).
[2] Harvard, x27.20.4F*; the proof of the letter-block, pfMS Typ 576 (79). The date of the gift is not recorded. Evidently, like Baron's Milton, the book was retained by the President of the College, but rather longer: it was finally turned over to the Library by President James Walker in 1875.
[3] An incomplete list of engravings commissioned by Hollis appears in *Memoirs*, pp. 502–3; even Blackburne was not fully aware of the extent of Hollis's activities.

Harvard collection show how carefully Hollis considered every detail and controlled its development.

Hollis's handling of his commissioned artists was typically generous and charming. He responded with genuine appreciation to the work they did, even though his eye was acutely critical and his ideas fixed. Having settled upon a subject and stipulated a fee, when the drawing or print was finished to his satisfaction Hollis paid at once, invariably adding an extra sum in gratitude. When the edition had been printed he sometimes returned the plate or block to the artist or to someone else who might benefit from having it; and on occasion he actually repurchased plates to have additional impressions made, even though he had borne the full expense to begin with. The *Diary* records many such transactions, but Hollis or his estate must have regained control, or at least temporary use, of most of these plates, for they were liberally used to illustrate Blackburne's *Memoirs*.

Hollis also paid for impressions that he furnished to publishers at no cost for the adornment of works he wished to promote, including publications sponsored by others. When Jonas Hanway proposed a new edition of a book about Hanway's favourite charity, the Marine Society, Hollis provided an engraved 'View of the Committee Room' at the Society, executed by Cipriani, whose name appears on it. We would not know of Hollis's connection were it not for his autograph annotation on a proof preserved in the Harvard collection.[1] He had learned magnanimity from Milton and through Thucydides he associated it with virtue and freedom, and he practised magnanimity without ostentation all his life.

Inevitably letterpress printing of several sorts was necessary for the execution of his Plan. At the simplest level this meant inducing the publishers of periodicals, notably the *St James's Chronicle* and the *London Chronicle*, to reprint articles deemed supportive of the ideals of freedom, or reporting gross violations of civil rights. From time to time Hollis made little gifts of five or ten guineas to the editors or publishers, never connected with any specific publication, but said to be 'for services to freedom'. The same journals also published a stream of pseudonymous letters from Hollis, mainly during the years 1764 to 1770. Their kaleidoscopic signatures present a fascinating array. We are on firm antiquarian ground with letters signed 'Patina Antiquarior' and

[1] Jonas Hanway *An Account of the Marine Society* 6th ed. (London 1759), plate inserted before sig. I1^r; proof in pfMS Typ 576 (6). Hollis is also listed as subscribing ten guineas to the charity, and possibly three guineas more noted as coming from 'T.H.'

dealing with such topics as cannon cast for Elizabeth I; but the political bias is only too clear in those signed 'Rerum Capitalium Vindex', 'One of the People', 'Roast Beef of Old England', 'No Blinker', 'A Friend to King George', 'Heart of Oak', 'Suum Cuique', and the like – one is tempted to run through the whole list. Some are reprinted in the appendices to the *Memoirs* for those who care to sample them; more are listed in the *Diary*; and I suspect that still more remain undetected in the pages of the newspapers. Hollis also undertook to supply other polemic writers to the journals, and to that end recruited the pseudonymous services of Francis Blackburne, Theophilus Lindsey, and Richard Baron, among others. He slipped in propaganda wherever he could: for example, when John Bell published *Bell's Common Place Book* (London 1770) modelled on John Locke's system, the examples that were included look suspiciously like Hollis's handiwork: quotations from Algernon Sidney, the periodical *The Old Whig*, and travel notes suggestive of his Grand Tour diaries, now lost.

A task that he considered still more important and began earlier was to rescue the substantive texts of the Commonwealth thinkers and propagandists, not only to make them available but to broadcast them: 'Ut spargam', as he wrote on numerous title-pages. Some were still to be found in their original editions in sufficient numbers in the bookshops, and these he purchased when he met with them, having them rebound or at any rate vamped to draw 'attention, with preservation' to them. But as his Plan developed he could see that he would be unable to spread them abroad freely enough by relying on finding copies of the old editions, and his sense of the market told him that new editions were unlikely to sell well enough to attract publishers. A solution had to be found.

By 1760, well launched into the execution of his Plan, Hollis was actively intervening in editing, printing, and publishing his chosen texts. His name never appeared in any of them. From the very beginning of the *Diary* in April 1759, one can see that he was already on familiar terms with many of the publishers, printers, and booksellers in London. Among the printers, three stand out. William Bowyer the younger, probably the most scholarly English printer of his time, not only printed editions to Hollis's order, but also produced the Latin translation of Hollis's preface to John Wallis, *Grammatica linguae anglicanae* (London 1765), a book that we shall see is of great importance in the Hollis canon. Bowyer was also persuaded after the Harvard fire of 1764 to give the College a copy of his own meticulous edition of the

Greek New Testament and commentary with a most complimentary inscription, bound in two volumes, black morocco, by John Shove.[1]

The other printers most often employed by Hollis were William Strahan, Senior and Junior, the latter towards the end of the sixties when he had unhappily quarrelled with his father. The younger Strahan afforded Hollis ready access to the pages of the *London Chronicle* for many letters and squibs; Hollis, for his part, was disturbed by the family rupture and tried, without much success, to bring father and son together again.

The publisher and bookseller most favoured by Hollis was Andrew Millar, a near neighbour in Pall Mall, who, at his suggestion in March 1760, reprinted two sermons by Jonathan Mayhew on the taking of Quebec. Thereafter Millar served as publisher, alone or in partnership with others, of numerous books sponsored by Hollis. Their dealings appear in many entries in the *Diary*, which (as usual) provides only a skeleton outline of most transactions.

One of their more influential joint ventures began in 1763, when Millar planned a trip to Scotland. Hollis had heard through Bishop Edmund Law of a powerful work called *The Confessional* attacking conformity to the Thirty-Nine Articles and other doctrinal rules of the Church of England, written some years earlier by Archdeacon Francis Blackburne, who was rector of Richmond in Yorkshire and a prebendary of Durham. Blackburne had never attempted to publish it, at least in part because he felt no publisher would undertake it. Such a book, of course, had both political and religious implications, and when it did appear, it ended Blackburne's chances for further ecclesiastical preferment.

Hollis asked Millar to call on Blackburne on his way through the Midlands to see if he could procure the manuscript for publication; it would appear that Hollis was prepared to underwrite the costs. Through this intervention its first edition was printed in 1766 by William Bowyer and published, without the name of the author, over the imprint of Samuel Bladon, an occasional associate of Millar. *The Confessional* brought on a furious pamphlet war in the North American

---

[1] Blackburne printed President Edward Holyoke's letter of thanks for the volumes, *Memoirs*, pp. 805–6, but lamented the absence of Bowyer's inscription. In volume 1 of the edition at Harvard, x 26.99*, it reads, 'Collegio Harvardensi, Novi Orbis Decori et Ornamento, Veteris Admirationi, Academiis Britannicis Virtute et Moribus non tam Aemulo quam Exemplo, Munusculum hoc donat Guilielmus Bowyer.' In 1767 Bowyer also presented a 1742 edition of Erasmus *Epistolae*.

colonies as well as in England, with contributors ranging from Archbishop Thomas Secker to such leading Dissenters as Caleb Fleming, and it went into a second edition in 1767 and a third in 1770 in order to answer some of the attacks it had provoked. The title-pages of all three editions exhibit signs of Hollis's influence.

Hollis bought numerous copies of all three editions to be put into emblematic bindings for wide distribution on both sides of the Atlantic. He communicated with its author principally through the Archdeacon's son-in-law, the Reverend Theophilus Lindsey. (Another of Blackburne's sons-in-law was the Reverend John Disney, who eventually inherited the Hollis estate.) Inexplicably, Hollis and Blackburne seem never to have actually met, and at first Hollis even mistook the minister's given name. But he immediately recognized and approved the principles Blackburne set forth, while Blackburne saw a kindred spirit in Hollis, and *The Confessional* was immensely influential in the political–theological struggle to relax High Church doctrines, an end achieved in neither man's lifetime. It was especially important in the colonists' fight to prevent Secker's plan of episcopizing the North American colonies. And when Thomas Brand Hollis decided that a *Memoir* of Thomas Hollis should be compiled and published, he delegated the task to Blackburne.

An interesting and complex undertaking began on 15 November 1764, when Millar agreed to reprint Henry Neville's *Plato redivivus*, a dialogue on government and the monarch that Hollis thought peculiarly appropriate in the early years of George III's reign. A week later Millar discovered that Robert Dodsley claimed to have 700 copies left of an edition with an introduction by Joseph Spence published in 1745 (a year in which it was also appropriate). The courtesy of the trade forbade another reprint while someone else held such a large remainder, so Hollis commissioned Millar to purchase the stock from Dodsley and reissue it with a new title-page and introduction.

Dodsley proved a hard bargainer, acting (as Hollis recorded) 'sordidly and perversely', and matters dragged on until 8 February 1765, when it turned out that the remainder consisted of only 300 copies, which Millar bought from Dodsley for £15. Hollis paid an additional £20 to Millar for his expenses and to cover the cost of printing cancels for the front matter. He himself wrote the new introduction, signing it modestly with his typographical liberty-cap instead of name or initials. When all was completed at the end of the month, Hollis bought twenty-four copies from Millar for special binding and distribution, despite the fact that he had already assumed the whole expense of the reissue.

Hollis remained on friendly terms with Millar until 12 May 1767. Millar's health had been slowly failing (he died in 1768), and that may possibly account for the intransigence that breached their relations. Early in 1767 Millar and Thomas Cadell had agreed to Hollis's proposal for an edition of 750 copies of the prose works of Milton in three volumes quarto, again edited by Richard Baron. By mid-May, Millar repudiated the agreement and said he would take only 150 copies in quarto and a further 500 in octavo, a change that would require a complete re-setting of the text. A trial sheet in royal quarto had already been printed by Bowyer. Hollis was outraged. He burned the sheet and abandoned the edition. Two days later he received a further communication from Millar denying that any agreement had existed, and saying he meant no offence, whereupon Hollis quoted Falstaff in his *Diary*, 'No abuse, Hal, no abuse!'

Other publishers appearing with more or less frequency were Lockyer Davis and Charles Reymers, Thomas Cadell, Thomas Davies, John Nourse (sometimes in partnership with Paul Vaillant), Robert and James Dodsley (despite the altercation over *Plato redivivus*), Samuel Bladon, William Johnston, Edmund and Charles Dilly, John Almon, and George Kearsley, the last two well-known publishers of radical literature. Still other names appear in Hollis imprints, but probably as part owners of copyrights, members of congers, or minor distributors; and more turn up in the *Diary*, but generally as proprietors of bookshops frequently visited.

The pattern established with Millar and some of the others, if indeed Hollis had not adopted it earlier, paralleled his treatment of graphic artists. He would choose a text and persuade a publisher to have it printed according to exacting standards. His persuasion might involve one or more of a series of familiar elements: outright subsidy, partial or full; the provision at no cost of a striking frontispiece; and editorial work and proofreading by himself or other reliable persons. His own editorial contributions were always anonymous, and he was deeply upset when his disguise was penetrated.[1]

Having essentially paid for the publication and its decoration, he would then actually purchase from the nominal publisher multiple

[1] As it was in the notice of Algernon Sidney's *Discourses Concerning Government* printed in the *Monthly Review* 29 (1763), p. 243; see *Diary* 3 and 30 November 1763.

copies in sheets to be specially bound for distribution, and add on top of that a cash bonus for having fallen in with his proposals. In many cases the margins of the copies were further embellished with notes, exhortations, and marks of emphasis in Hollis's own hand. The *Diary* records many long days and evenings spent in such activities. The pattern was often repeated. More than thirty publications had Hollis's full or partial backing over a period of ten or twelve years, and the last of them was published late in 1773 with an imprint dated 1774. Not all were canonical texts. Hollis had a redeeming sense of humour: some were *jeux d'esprit* by favourite authors, like Henry Neville's *Isle of Pines* and *Parlament of Ladies*, both published in small editions in 1768, after the *London Chronicle* had declined to print them in its columns on the grounds of indecency.

The SPAC appears likely to have furnished a motive for a new and agreeable foray into the arts of the book: typographical design. I have mentioned his friendship with the aged Joseph Ames, from whom he apparently learned much about early books. He also knew and admired one of the deans of continental bibliography, Gerard Meerman, and gave to Harvard in 1766 a copy of Meerman's *Origines typographiae* (The Hague 1765), appropriately inscribed with a quotation from *Areopagitica* and a note of praise for Meerman's own 'NOBLE' library.[1] The book had been presented to Hollis by Meerman himself.

Hollis was inspired to combine his own interest in typography with his life-long study of classical antiquities, in particular numismatic inscriptions and other Latin epigraphy. To find the sources of his inspiration we have only to turn to such works as Antonio Agostini *Dialoghi. . . intorno alle medaglie, inscrittioni ed altre antichita* (Rome [1592?]) and Raphael Fabretti *Inscriptionum antiquarum. . . explicatio* (Rome 1702), among a cluster of such works that he presented to Harvard.[2] Whether he derived his style from these and similar books or from his memory of classical objects and his personal collection of antiquities is beside the point. He evidently found standard English typography of his period cluttered and fussy, and determined to bring classical simplicity to it.

Hollis approached a title-page exactly as he might have approached an inscription to be cut in stone. Like the classical models he admired, he used good roman capitals, usually all of one size, breaking away from the typographical complexity of many eighteenth-century title-pages. His use of punctuation was as sparse as he could manage. He sometimes

---

[1] Harvard, B 4057.765*.   [2] Harvard, Arc 1350.2F* and Class 6481.2F*.

THE ISLE OF PINES.

Or a late difcovery of a fourth Ifland, in
Terra Auftralis Incognita.

Being a true Relation of certain Englifh Perfons, who, in the days of Q. Elizabeth,
making a Voyage to the Eaft India, were caft
away, and wrecked upon that Ifland, and all
drowned, except one Man and four Women,
whereof one was a Negro. And now lately,
A. D. 1667, a Dutch fhip driven by foul
weather there, by chance have found their
Pofterity, fpeaking good Englifh, to amount
to 10 or 12,000 perfons, as they fuppofe.
The whole relation follows, written by the
Man himfelf a little before his death, and
declared to the Dutch by his grandchild.

[BY HENRY NEVILLE]

LONDON
PRINTED MDCLXVIII
REPRINTED FOR T. CADELL
MDCCLXVIII

THE PARLAMENT OF LADIES.

Or divers remarkable Orders, of the Ladies,
at Spring Garden, in Parlament affembled.
Together with certain Votes, of the unlaw-
ful Affembly, at Kate's, in Covent Garden.
Both fent abroad to prevent mifinformation.

[BY HENRY NEVILLE]

LONDON
PRINTED MDCXXXXVII
REPRINTED FOR T. CADELL
MDCCLXVIII

42   Title of Henry Neville's *The Isle of Pines* designed and sponsored by Thomas Hollis (page size, 17 × 10.4 cm)

43   Title of Henry Neville's *The Parlament of Ladies* designed and sponsored by Thomas Hollis (page size, 17 × 10.4 cm)

adopted the inscriptional custom of placing full stops between words at the normal height of hyphens, just as he did on the lettering-pieces of the bindings he commissioned, and indeed as he customarily wrote his own initials, 'T·H'.

He used his epigraphic style in the letterpress presentation label he inserted in some of his early gifts to Harvard. When he found that his gifts were customarily marked by the insertion of the college book-plate engraved by Nathaniel Hurd, filled out in manuscript, he commissioned an unidentified London engraver to cut a close imitation of

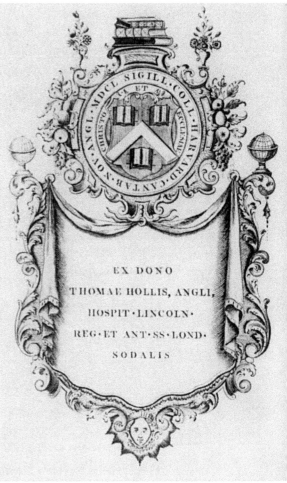

EX DONO
THOMAE HOLLIS, ANGLI,
HOSPIT · LINCOLN ·
REG · ET ANT · SS · LOND ·
SODALIS

44   Engraved bookplate by Nathaniel Hurd filled out in MS; Hollis's letterpress gift label; bookplate engraved in London for Hollis and printed in New England

Hurd's design with an engraved inscription copying the letterpress label. The metal plate was sent to Harvard in August 1767, and impressions from it were struck for his gifts to the college until it wore out, when it was replaced for a time by a vastly inferior line-block version.

Hollis liked the appearance of solid masses of type on the page, surrounded by plenty of white space. His influence on the typography of the text is less marked, but here, too, he is known to have preferred simplicity, and was among those who broke away from the earlier custom of capitalizing nouns in the middle of sentences. In this he was not alone; the tide of taste was already running strongly in that direction.

We can safely assume his designer's hand in books that he subsidized, or whose publication he strongly supported. In some other books in which he had no direct personal interest his intervention is documented by the *Diary* or other sources. Some cases are not so clear: were they imitation by someone who admired the style, or had he been consulted? Printers who had followed his instructions, and especially Bowyer, may well have employed the model in other publications in which Hollis did not participate. The *Memoirs*, six years after his death, was appropriately carried out in his own style.

One of the first publications in which he brought his ideas to bear appears to be the yearbook of the SPAC for 1760. The records of the Society show that in 1758 he worked with James Stuart on a medal for the Society based on Stuart's design. Several figures on the medal are near cousins of Hollis's favourite symbols. The yearbook for 1760 combines on its title and divisional titles an engraving by Basire of Stuart's medal and letterpress of unusual classical elegance, epigraphic in design. The typographer is not identified, but on the basis of later publications undoubtedly emanating from Hollis I have little hesitation in ascribing it to him. It is laid out in what he termed a 'simply inscripted manner', or, elsewhere, 'my own simple style'. At least through 1766 the Society continued to use the same typographical layout.[1]

A brief list of books that Hollis 'published, or procured to be published' appears on pp. 501–2 of the *Memoirs*, but it is not complete. Still more can be found through entries in the *Diary*, and others have been identified by Professor Robbins. Similarity of design and coincidence of trade publisher point to still more; some, of course, may be imitations.

---

[1] *Diary* 6 August 1765, 29 January 1766, and other places. See plate 45.

PREMIUMS

OFFERED BY THE SOCIETY INSTITUTED

AT LONDON FOR THE ENCOURAGEMENT

OF ARTS MANUFACTURES AND

COMMERCE.

By deeds of peace!

PAR·REG·

LONDON:

PRINTED BY ORDER OF THE SOCIETY.

MDCCLXI.

45   SPAC premium list. Medal
designed by James Stuart; typography
probably by Hollis, and with his
autograph inscription (page size,
20.1 × 11.6 cm)

A short selection, far from exhaustive, may carry conviction about Hollis's typographical activities. As we have seen, the yearbook of the SPAC continued the inscriptional style unchanged at least from 1760 to 1766. Also in 1760 is the *Proceedings of the Committee. . . for Cloathing French Prisoners of War*, the publication for which Hollis did indeed persuade Samuel Johnson to write an introduction, and paid him five guineas for doing so; and Rudyer Josip Boscovič's Newtonian poem in Latin, a publication for which Hollis was certainly responsible, though the title-page is somewhat conventional.[1]

In 1761 came the reprint of John Toland's life of Milton, with one unhappy flaw in its design – the use of capital U for V two-thirds of the way down the title-page. In 1762 appeared Vincenzio Martinelli's edition of the *Decamerone* of Boccaccio, with an engraved frontispiece almost certainly by Cipriani and probably commissioned by Hollis. A copy in the possession of the present writer was bound by John Shove. The *Diary* is curiously silent about the portrait and the publication in general, except for recording Hollis's advice to Martinelli (who followed it) on several points of annotation; but the family resemblance to other publications sponsored and designed by Hollis is unmistakable. Its royal quarto format and inscriptional title-page set the pattern for a series that continued next year with Sidney's *Discourses Concerning Government*, with Hollis as unacknowledged editor and a liberty-print as frontispiece. In 1764 came Locke's *Two Treatises on Government*, its lengthy imprint indicating widely dispersed distribution through the trade, and with a Cipriani portrait especially cut for it. Both the imprint (with one small variation) and the portrait recur in the 1765 edition of *Letters Concerning Toleration*. Seldom has an imprint with such a lengthy list of booksellers appeared more tolerable than in this inscriptional style.

Also in 1764, though its title is dated 1765, appeared John Wallis's *Grammatica*, already cited as a key to Hollis's plan of publication and distribution. He had reached several important conclusions. First, English was the language of liberty, because the great texts of the Commonwealth writers to which he constantly returned were liberty's finest expression; and second, those texts should be broadcast not only in England but throughout Europe. Wallis provided the means to make English accessible to any properly educated foreigner; therefore his book must be reprinted and widely circulated. Hollis furnished a

---

[1] *Diary* 30 August 1760, recording his persuasion of Millar to join Dodsley in its publication. It will be recalled that Samuel Johnson also befriended Boscovič, but took no effectual steps to help him find a publisher.

PROCEEDINGS OF THE COMMITTEE

APPOINTED TO MANAGE THE CONTRIBUTIONS

BEGUN AT LONDON DEC. XVIII MDCCLVIIII

FOR CLOATHING FRENCH PRISONERS OF WAR.

HOMO SVM: HVMANI NIHIL À ME ALIENVM PVTO.   TER.

L O N D O N

PRINTED BY ORDER OF THE COMMITTEE

MDCCLX,

46   *Proceedings of the Committee . . . for Cloathing French Prisoners of War.*
Title designed by Thomas Hollis (page size, 30.4 × 18.8 cm)

THE LIFE OF

IOHN MILTON;

Containing, befides

the hiftory of his works,

feveral extraordinary characters

of men, and books, fects, parties, and opinions :

WITH

AMYNTOR;

Or a defenfe of Milton's life :

BY IOHN TOLAND.

AND UARIOUS NOTES NOW ADDED.

VICTRIX CAUSA DIIS PLACVIT, SED VICTA CATONI.

LONDON PRINTED FOR IOHN DARBY MDCXCIX.

REPRINTED FOR A. MILLAR IN THE STRAND

MDCCLXI.

47   Hollis's edition of Toland (page size, 20.4 × 12.5 cm)

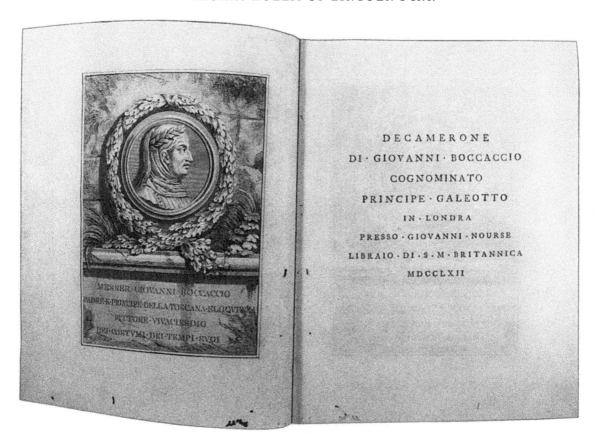

DECAMERONE
DI · GIOVANNI · BOCCACCIO
COGNOMINATO
PRINCIPE · GALEOTTO
IN · LONDRA
PRESSO · GIOVANNI · NOURSE
LIBRAIO · DI · S · M · BRITANNICA
MDCCLXII

48 Vincenzio Martinelli's edition of the *Decamerone*, designed and
probably sponsored by Hollis, with frontispiece engraved by Cipriani
(page size, 27.6 × 21.5 cm)

frontispiece portrait by Cipriani, and attempted to persuade Bishop
Robert Lowth to write a learned preface. When Lowth declined, Hollis
himself undertook the task and asked William Bowyer to translate it into
Latin. Then he decided to rewrite the preface to include Wallis's
recollections of the founding of the Royal Society, so that Bowyer once
more had to work on it, and the book as published has a multi-page (and
nearly undetectable) cancel in the preliminaries. Both versions of the
preface survive only in Hollis's own copy (now in the collection of the
present writer), which also bears his autograph annotation ending 'The
Catalogue, a whim, was drawn up by me'. This 'Catalogus librorum
apud A. Millar', which occupies both sides of the last leaf, is Hollis's
bibliography of the literature of liberty; a whim indeed! Perhaps the

96

whim is embodied in the fact, coyly confessed in a letter to the elder Pitt of 9 March 1765, that three of the books in it had not yet been reprinted as claimed.[1] By combining this catalogue with the list of books drawn up by Hollis for the enlightenment of the Swedish people in 1772 to encourage them to resist Gustavus III's *coup d'état* with its ensuing autocracy,[2] Professor Caroline Robbins was able to reconstruct with some assurance the 'Library of Liberty', as she properly called it.[3]

The *Grammatica* was printed, partly if not chiefly at Hollis's expense, in an edition of eight hundred, of which he promptly bought back one hundred copies in sheets, which he turned over to Matthewman for symbolic binding in red morocco, smoke prints and all. These were sent, mostly anonymously, all over England and through Europe from Uppsala to Malta and from Portugal to Moscow. Several also reached North America. It is *almost* a publisher's binding, and although there is no record to confirm it, one suspects that when the first hundred were exhausted Hollis bought and bound still more. Has anyone ever seen a copy in a contemporary binding *not* executed by Matthewman for Hollis? After Millar's death in 1768, his widow found a small remainder, presumably in sheets, and sold it to Benjamin White of Fleet Street, another bookseller acquaintance of Hollis, but no more is heard of it. It can scarcely have been a popular book except in Hollis's terms.

There is no need to list here all the books sponsored by Hollis, but one more surely deserves mention because it demonstrates so clearly his great concern with the looming conflict between the North American colonies and the mother country. This is *The True Sentiments of America* (London 1768), compiled and edited by Hollis and published for him by John Almon, with a title-page in the familiar inscriptional style. It is made up of current resolutions of the House of Representatives of the Massachusetts Bay Colony, letters and petitions sent by the colonists to His Majesty's ministers in England, and a reprint of the anonymous *Dissertation on the Canon and the Feudal Law*, ascribed by Hollis to Jeremiah Gridley but actually written by the young John Adams.

Hollis selected the contents of this book from the newspapers and cuttings supplied to him by his faithful Boston correspondent, the Reverend Andrew Eliot. Its purpose was to emphasize the basic loyalty of the colonists while exposing their grievances and the difficulties under

---

[1] Original in Public Record Office, G.D. 8/40.
[2] First printed in *London Chronicle* 6-8 October 1772; reprinted in *Memoirs*, pp. 659–60. It is worth remarking that a number of the books in this list are seventeenth-century editions, not reprinted in the eighteenth century.   [3] See above, note 3 p. 29.

John Eliot

THE TRVE SENTIMENTS OF AMERICA:
CONTAINED IN A COLLECTION OF LETTERS SENT FROM THE HOVSE OF REPRESENTATIVES OF THE PROVINCE OF MASSACHVSETTS BAY TO SEVERAL PERSONS OF HIGH RANK IN THIS KINGDOM:

TOGETHER
WITH CERTAIN PAPERS RELATING TO A SVPPOSED LIBEL ON THE GOVERNOR OF THAT PROVINCE, AND A DISSERTATION ON THE CANON AND THE FEVDAL LAW.

LONDON; PRINTED FOR I. ALMON, IN PICCADILLY.
1768.

49 Hollis's compilation *The True Sentiments of America*, based on materials sent him by the Reverend Andrew Eliot; copy presented to Eliot, with his heir's signature on title (page size, 20.6 × 12.4 cm)

which they laboured, in an effort to alter the course of governmental policy before events reached a critical stage. That it failed to do so was one of the sources of the pessimism clouding Hollis's later years, leading him eventually to retire from London with the feeling that his 'little Powers of action among the Great' had indeed been exhausted.

But Hollis did not confine his support to publications that he himself sponsored. When he found a modern work to his liking, he would step in and take a hand in keeping it before the public. An example is Bishop Richard Hurd's *Moral and Political Dialogues*, first published in 1759. Hollis's intervention is evident in the inscriptional style of both the title-page and the dedication leaf of the third edition, 1765. In the same year he was similarly involved in the second editions of two books by James Harris, *Hermes* and *Three Treatises*, published by Nourse and Vaillant. Catherine Macaulay's Whig *History of England* so pleased him that he designed the title-pages from the second edition onward, and also, at her husband's request, planned a portrait frontispiece to be engraved, modelling it on a coin of Marcus Brutus in his own cabinet.[1] Typography, engraving, and layout closely resemble those of Martinelli's Boccaccio. When Edward and Charles Dilly reprinted the *History* in octavo in 1769, they copied the typography and reversed the portrait in accommodating it to the new format. At least one other work by Mrs Macaulay, *Loose Remarks on Certain Positions to be Found in Mr. Hobbes's Philosophical Rudiments of Government and Society* (London 1767), was designed in both octavo (first edition) and quarto (second edition) by Hollis, with his typographical liberty-cap on the title-page.

Matters in other parts of the world also engaged Hollis's attention and resulted in publications. Early in 1769 he bought a member's share in the East India Company, and on 27 July he recorded, 'At a General Court of the East India Company, being the first which has been held since I became a Member of that Company. The Company is now, clearly, a gaming, political Company, but the proceedings relating to it are most curious and important. I am glad to have taken a share in it, however it may turn out in regard to profit, and though only it should exercise my Understanding and Judgment.'

During subsequent weeks he attended meeting after meeting of the Company, and found no reason to change his view of its proceedings. He also began combing the bookstores for tracts relating to India and East Indian affairs; as usual, he knew what he was looking for. On 6 September he found a prime desideratum. 'With Mr. Cadel. Paid him

[1] Sommer (cited above, note 1 p. 75), pp. 142–3 and plates 8, 9, 10.

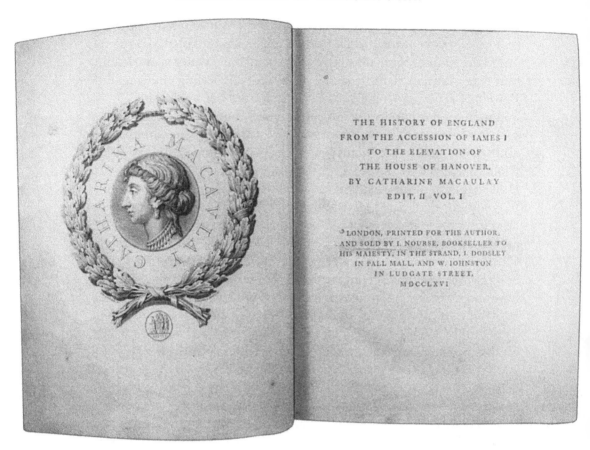

THE HISTORY OF ENGLAND
FROM THE ACCESSION OF IAMES I
TO THE ELEVATION OF
THE HOUSE OF HANOVER.
BY CATHARINE MACAULAY
EDIT. II VOL I

LONDON, PRINTED FOR THE AUTHOR,
AND SOLD BY I. NOURSE, BOOKSELLER TO
HIS MAIESTY, IN THE STRAND, I. DODSLEY
IN PALL MALL, AND W. IOHNSTON
IN LUDGATE STREET,
MDCCLXVI

50   Catherine Macaulay's *History of England*. Title designed by Hollis,
who also commissioned Cipriani's emblematic frontispiece (page size,
27.6 × 21.1 cm)

10/6, for a *very scarce* tract, written by Luke Scrafton, which was
obtained by his means. Three and four Guineas have been paid for this
tract.' On 20 September he took the next step. 'With Mr. Kearsley, at
Wills C[offee]. H[ouse].; when it was agreed, that the very scarce tract
of Mr. Scrafton's, should be reprinted in a handsome manner by Mr.
William Strahan jun., from my copy of it, for the benefit of G. Kearsley
and T. Cadell.' Later entries in the *Diary* record consultations with
Strahan and Kearsley about the progress of the tract, until on 24
October he wrote, 'With Mr. Kearsley. Paid him 18s. for nine copies of
the new edit. of Mr. Scrafton's pamphlet, intitled, "Reflections on the
government of Indostan; with a short sketch of the history of Bengal,
from 1738 to 1756: and an account of the English affairs to 1758" . . . At
home . . . Busied in preparing copies of Mr. Scrafton's tract for

LOOSE
REMARKS

ON

CERTAIN POSITIONS to be found in

Thomas

Mr. HOBBES's Philoſophical Rudiments

OF

GOVERNMENT and SOCIETY.

With a SHORT SKETCH of

A DEMOCRATICAL Form of Government,

In a LETTER to Signior PAOLI.

by Catharine Macaulay

LONDON:

Printed for T. DAVIES, in Ruſſel-ſtreet, Covent-garden;
ROBINSON and ROBERTS, in Pater-noſter Row; and
T. CADELL, in the Strand.

MDCCLXVII.

51   Catherine Macaulay's *Loose Remarks* on Hobbes; first (octavo)
edition. Sponsored by Thomas Hollis; note his typographical liberty-
cap (page size, 20.7 × 12 cm)

LOOSE REMARKS ON CERTAIN POSITIONS
TO BE FOUND IN MR. HOBBES'
PHILOSOPHICAL RUDIMENTS OF
GOVERNMENT AND SOCIETY
WITH A SHORT SKETCH OF A
DEMOCRATICAL FORM OF GOVERNMENT
IN A LETTER TO SIGNIOR PAOLI
BY CATHARINE MACAULAY
THE SECOND EDITION
WITH TWO LETTERS
ONE FROM AN AMERICAN GENTLEMAN
TO THE AUTHOR WHICH CONTAINS
SOME COMMENTS ON HER SKETCH OF THE
DEMOCRATICAL FORM OF GOVERNMENT
AND THE AUTHOR'S ANSWER.

LONDON
PRINTED FOR W. JOHNSTON IN LUDGATE-STREET.
T. DAVIES IN RUSSEL-STREET COVENT-GARDEN.
E. AND C. DILLY IN THE POULTRY. J. ALMON IN
PICCADILLY. ROBINSON AND ROBERTS IN PATER-
NOSTER ROW. AND T. CADELL IN THE STRAND.
MDCCLXIX.

52   Catherine Macaulay's *Loose Remarks* on Hobbes; second edition.
Designed and sponsored by Hollis; note his typographic liberty-cap
(page size, 27 × 20.8 cm)

dispersion.' The layout of the title-page is obviously Hollis's design: and, as usual in such matters, he had not only sponsored the publication, he also purchased copies from the booksellers whom he had encouraged.

Another interesting case is *A Complete Collection of the Genuine Papers, Letters, &c. in the Case of John Wilkes* (1769), printed in London despite its Berlin imprint. The text had been published earlier in Paris. The 'Berlin' edition looks suspiciously like Hollis's handiwork, and its organization resembles that of *The True Sentiments of America*: a series of short letters or sections followed by a longer piece, in this case a reprint of No. 45 of *The North Briton*. Although there is no reference to this book in the *Diary*, Hollis took more than ordinary interest in the Wilkes case. He was repelled by Wilkes when they first met in 1759, but the celebrated Middlesex election scandal of nearly a decade later was a different matter: it involved parliamentary corruption, civil liberties, and free elections, all subjects dear to his heart. In the absence of direct proof, however, the connection with Hollis can only be regarded as a possibility. Indeed, he may have taken a cue for *The True Sentiments* from the organization of the Wilkes papers.

The last imposing quarto in the 'simple' style came out two years after Hollis left London, Algernon Sidney's *Works* (1772); while two small tracts of Hollis's old friend the Reverend Theophilus Lindsey, first of Dorset and latterly of Catterick in Yorkshire, bear the mark of his design. Although they are dated 1774, they were actually published late in 1773.

Evidence that his skill and taste as a designer was known and respected is not lacking. We cannot be absolutely sure in the case of one monumental book, James Stuart's *The Antiquities of Athens* i (London 1762). Its title-page has a decidedly Hollisian look, despite its uncharacteristic use of ornaments. But Stuart and Hollis were close friends, and Hollis not only subscribed to its publication but also gave Stuart permission to reproduce pictures of two Greek owls from his collection, with the stipulation that one should be recorded as belonging to Thomas Brand. (This Stuart failed to do.) There is a possible case for Hollis's intervention, or at least influence in the design; it may also be thought that the influence was mutual.

Hollis was an early subscriber to Robert Adam's imposing *Ruins of the Palace of the Emperor Diocletian at Spalatro*, another of the heralds of the neo-classical revival. He had met Adam soon after the architect came to London from Scotland, and he admired Adam's work. The great book was long in appearing. Hollis's *Diary* records a last minute consultation by the printer, William Strahan, Jr, on 6 December 1763, to design 'the

REFLECTIONS

ON THE GOVERNMENT OF INDOSTAN.

WITH A SHORT SKETCH

OF THE HISTORY OF BENGAL,

FROM MDCCXXXVIIII TO MDCCLVI;

AND AN ACCOVNT

OF THE ENGLISH AFFAIRS

TO MDCCLVIII:

BY LVKE SCRAFTON ESQ.

LONDON, PRINTED MDCCLXIII

REPRINTED BY W. STRAHAN IVN.

FOR G. KEARSLEY, IN LVDGATE STREET,

AND T. CADELL, IN THE STRAND,

MDCCLXX

53 *Reflections on the Government of Indostan,* designed and sponsored by Hollis (page size, 20.7 × 12.7 cm)

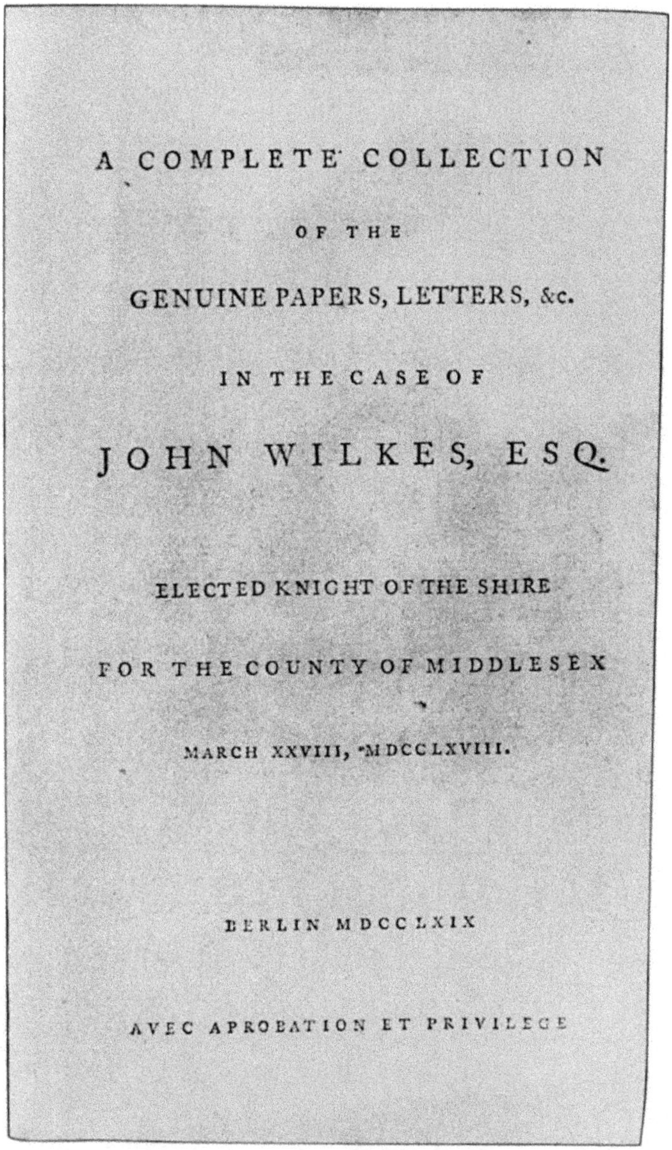

A COMPLETE COLLECTION

OF THE

GENUINE PAPERS, LETTERS, &c.

IN THE CASE OF

JOHN WILKES, ESQ.

ELECTED KNIGHT OF THE SHIRE

FOR THE COUNTY OF MIDDLESEX

MARCH XXVIII, MDCCLXVIII.

BERLIN MDCCLXIX

AVEC APROBATION ET PRIVILEGE

54 Wilkes Papers, actually published in London; possibly designed
and/or sponsored by Hollis (page size, 15 × 9 cm)

RVINS OF THE PALACE
OF THE EMPEROR DIOCLETIAN
AT SPALATRO IN DALMATIA
BY R· ADAM F·R·S F·S·A
ARCHITECT TO THE KING
AND TO THE QVEEN
PRINTED FOR THE AVTHOR
MDCCLXIIII

55   *Ruins of the Palace of the Emperor Diocletian at Spalatro,* by Robert
Adam. Title designed by Hollis (page size, 51.3 × 36.8 cm)

Title of a book... after the manner of an antient inscription, which was settled accordingly'. Next day Strahan returned, to exhibit the last proof of the design, and so Adam's masterpiece was published with a Hollis title-page.

Books were not the only kind of graphic art for which his opinion was sought and followed. Cipriani consulted him about designs to be painted on George III's coronation coach, and Hollis was a member of the committee appointed by the SPAC to design a coronation guinea; the Hollis papers at Harvard contain several sheets of trial sketches. Joseph Nollekens, as we have seen, consulted him about a bas-relief in 1761, and Jonas Hanway about a proper inscription for a portrait of George III, settling on the words 'SALVS POPVLORVM'. Thomas Pingo, expert medallist and die-cutter though he was, consulted about the inscription for a coronation medal for the King of Poland, as well as designs for a medal for the Bishop of Osnaburgh and one for George III to present to the Royal Military Academy, Woolwich. In the last case, Hollis's ideas did not prevail, and a design said to be vastly inferior was adopted instead. In 1760 Andrew Millar sought Hollis's advice about the design of a frontispiece for his projected edition of the works of James Thomson, and in the next year Millar asked for his help in composing and designing a suitable inscription for a memorial to the poet.

The most unexpected design consultation of all, and perhaps the one with longest-lasting effect, began only a little more than a year before Hollis abandoned London for the peace of his Dorset farms. On 11 May 1769 he recorded a visit to Wedgwood's in Great Newport Street to view the newly introduced Etruscan ware. He was sadly disappointed, pronouncing it 'a very imperfect imitation' of the ancient prototypes. As it happened, Josiah Wedgwood was Hollis's near neighbour in St James's Square,[1] and the two must also have known each other as fellow members of more than one learned society.

At any rate, on 4 April 1770 Hollis took another look at the Etruscan ware and was again dissatisfied. Two days later, Wedgwood and his partner Thomas Bentley called on Hollis for a consultation and to see the genuine Etruscan ware in his miniature museum, to which they paid another visit a few days later. Wedgwood and Bentley decided to take Hollis's advice in the matter. At his suggestion, they engaged Cipriani to draw designs for them according to the antique models, and thus the last piece of designing in which Hollis was engaged before he retired from London resulted in patterns that have been familiar ever since.

---

[1] H. B. Wheatley *London Past and Present* (London 1891), p. 302.

4

'Ut spargam'

THE AIM of the first chapter was to describe the Miltonian education of Thomas Hollis V and his development into a liberal Whig – not a party man, but a Whig with a difference: one who shunned overt political office or alliance, or personal advancement, a man who wished to do his utmost to promote the ideals of civil and religious freedom while remaining as nearly invisible as possible. Some of the means he employed appeared in the second and third chapters. He bound chosen texts in a form that would draw attention to them and increase their chance of survival. In addition, he subsidized their publication, saw to it that they appeared with suitably dignified typography, and provided means to make them accessible to non-English-speaking persons. All this activity would have availed little without one final step: making sure that the liberty-prints and canonical texts reached their intended audience.

His distribution of prints in May and June of 1762 affords a particularly good example, because Hollis was more than usually specific in listing recipients in the *Diary* entries for 22 May and 1 and 30 June, naming slightly more than seventy individuals in England to whom they were sent, beginning with William Pitt and Mr Speaker Onslow. Among a host of others we may note Catherine Macaulay, Mark Akenside, Horace Walpole, David Garrick, Sir William Chambers, James Stuart, Tobias Smollett, Sir Joshua Reynolds, William Hogarth, Owen Ruffhead, Allan Ramsay, Dr Matthew Maty, Dr Thomas Birch, and Dr Anthony Askew – a broad spectrum of recipients, to say the least. Still more were dispersed on the continent and in the New World, and others were presented to libraries and other institutions.

The liberty books like Harrington, Milton, Nedham, Sidney, Locke, and Wallis's *Grammatica* were even more widely distributed. Hollis employed agents and consular offices all over Europe to see that they went to private persons from Linnaeus in Sweden to the Prince of Torremuzza in Sicily; to libraries in Uppsala, Copenhagen, Moscow, Berlin, Göttingen, Wittenberg, Wolfenbüttel, Switzerland, Austria,

Italy, Spain, Portugal, and various cities in the Low Countries; and to learned societies from the Academy in St Petersburg to the Accademia della Crusca in Florence. All or most of these gifts were purportedly anonymous, inscribed to their recipients by 'an Englishman, a Citizen of the World'.

Naturally enough his support was most generous to libraries, because through them he felt he had at least a chance of reaching a wider public. His gifts were not restricted to books whose publication he had advanced, or even necessarily to books with which he sympathized. Hollis was a firm believer in the principle that truth will triumph, and did not hesitate to donate texts that preached views the exact opposite of his own convictions. The most notable instance was his gift of a large collection of Jesuit books to the public library at Zürich;[1] he was confident that in the event their texts would defeat their own purpose.

More in line with his own ideas, he sent upwards of four hundred volumes, carefully chosen to illuminate the theme of civil and religious freedom, many of them finely bound, to the public library at Bern. There they remain together as a collection to this day, a striking sight in the handsome bookcase built to preserve them.[2] His confidential agent in Switzerland, Rodolph de Valtravers (or Vautravers) kept his secret so well that the donor was unknown until after Hollis's death. Valtravers also transmitted back to Hollis the official thanks of the Senate of the Republic of Bern to their unknown English benefactor. As we have seen, when Hollis's bequest brought a small sum of money for Bern to buy additional books for the collection, a local binder had imitations of several Hollis tools cut so that books so acquired might be similarly decorated. Likewise at Zürich, books bought with a gift of money from Hollis were stamped with tools imitating his own.

In England, Christ's College, Cambridge, was a particular object of benefaction because it had been Milton's college. One may suspect that Hollis's afternoons of conversation with such persons as Joseph Ames and various knowledgeable booksellers had stood him in good stead, for he gave the College Library precisely the four most important variants of the first edition of *Paradise Lost* together with the second edition of 1674 and the third of 1678; the 1645 *Poems* 'elegantly bound' and containing the engraved frontispiece; and various other Miltoniana,

---

[1] *Memoirs*, pp. 169, 171, 189–90, 418, 744–5.

[2] *Memoirs* pp. 68–72, 242, 247–9, 266–7, 739–43. The collection is discussed and analysed at length by Hans Utz in his excellent monograph *Die Hollis–Sammlung in Bern* (Bern [1959]).

including the bust now in the Senior Combination Room. Other gifts included a selection of the canonical texts, works on numismatics and classical antiquities, a run of liberty-prints, and most important of all, a copy of the 1698 edition of Locke on government that he had come upon in a London bookshop and found to contain autograph notes and revisions by Locke himself and by his French translator, Pierre Coste.[1] Benefactions elsewhere in Cambridge included a portrait of Sir Isaac Newton by Enoch Seeman given to Newton's college, Trinity, in October 1761,[2] and a crayon portrait of Oliver Cromwell that Hollis ascribed to Alexander Cooper and gave to Cromwell's college, Sidney Sussex, in 1766.[3]

In London a natural object of Hollis's bounty was the great collection of Dissenting literature, Dr Williams's Library, situated in Hollis's day in Red Cross Street, Cripplegate. The self-defeating quality of Hollis's anonymity is splendidly illustrated at Dr Williams's. All the inquirer need do is to examine the manuscript book of accessions for 1760 and the years immediately following, and to call for every volume listed as coming 'from an anonymous hand'. Every one of them is from Hollis, many in emblematic bindings by Matthewman. All other donors appear to have been quite willing to be named. The Royal Society and the Society of Antiquaries received appropriate gifts from Hollis in smaller numbers, but for them he also served in the more useful role of transmitter of important works by continental authors, particularly in the field of antiquarian research.

Hollis the patriot was a supporter of the newly founded British Museum, giving books, manuscripts, and antiquities, although the Trustees did not always seem properly grateful. In 1761 their Committee rejected 'a rare and master-print against the Jesuits' as likely to give offence; Hollis's gift had been contingent upon a promise to keep it on display. It was gladly accepted by Christ's College, to which he next offered it.[4] Hollis thought the Museum's response 'strange, most strange', and as a direct consequence he gave the collection of Jesuit books, mentioned earlier, to Zürich rather than to the new national library. But he was not deterred from making other gifts to the Museum, including a large collection of tracts on the controversy surrounding Archdeacon Blackburne's book, *The Confessional*. Perhaps his most interesting gift was a manuscript that he found in Edward Ballard's

---

[1] *Diary* 20 April 1764.   [2] *Diary* 29 October 1761.   [3] *Diary* 15 January 1766.
[4] *Diary* 6 and 12 January, 21 August 1761.

bookshop in Little Britain, containing themes or exercises in Greek and Latin in the handwriting of Edward VI.[1]

Of far greater consequence to the Museum was his intermediacy in major donations by two other persons. Hollis was assisted in the management of his personal funds by a trusted stockbroker, Solomon da Costa, an elderly Jewish merchant who had emigrated from Amsterdam as a very young man in 1704. Da Costa was not only an excellent man of affairs; he was also a scholar and a generous benefactor of both Jewish and Christian charities. Like many before and since, he was grateful to his adopted country for providing a haven from persecution where individual enterprise might prosper.

Early in his English career he had come upon a superb collection of Hebrew books and manuscripts, splendidly bound in red morocco for Charles II, with his cipher, by the King's Binder. Charles neither took delivery nor paid for them; John Evelyn saw them, still at the binder's, in 1689. Da Costa bought them *en bloc* for his own use about 1720,[2] and in 1759, when he decided to present them to the nation, he turned to his friend Hollis to put into suitably dignified English his letter offering them to the Trustees. His gift was gratefully accepted, and it forms one of the foundation-stones of the Museum's Hebrew collection.

An even more significant transaction first appears in the *Diary* for 1761 under the date of October 18:

M[r]. Kent [otherwise unidentified, but possibly Henry Kent, printer to the City of London] with me for a couple of hours, and left with me a Mss account 'of a most curious & important collection of *all* the books & pamphlets printed from the beginning of the year 1641 to the Coronation of King Charles the second 1661; and near one hundred Manuscripts never yet in print; the whole containing 30,000 books & tracts, uniformly bound, consisting of 2000 volumes, dated in the most exact manner, & so carefully preserved as to have received no damage. The catalogue of them makes 12 Vol. in folio, & they are so marked & numbered, that the least Tract may be readily found, & even the very day on which they became public, wrote on most of them.' – which collection, M[r]. Kent is informed is now to be sold, as he apprehends, for a trifling consideration, & has been offered, as he hears, to the Earl of Bute: but he has not been informed either of the name of the

---

[1] *Diary* 25 February, 10 March 1763.

[2] *Memoirs*, Appendix v, pp. 613–15; Edward Edwards *Lives of the Founders of the British Museum* (London and New York 1870), pp. 328–30, with an eloquent appreciation of Da Costa's life and many philanthropies; Arundel Esdaile *The British Museum Library* (London [1946]), pp. 48, 179–80, 297, 373; Nicolas Barker *et al. Treasures of the British Library* ([London] 1988), pp. 38, 64, 142, 147, 210. Edwards, Esdaile, and Barker were evidently unaware of Hollis's participation.

Person who made the Collection, or who owns it now. MEM. To inquire farther about this Matter, which may be of importance, & to procure the Collection, if possible, some how for the public.

Of course these were the Thomason Tracts, the backbone of our knowledge of the ephemeral literature of the Commonwealth period. What part Hollis actually played in the subsequent negotiations is obscured by his habitual self-effacement, but it seems probable that at the very least he was a quiet propagandist behind the scenes, no doubt pressing for their acquisition by the nation through his connections in the learned societies.[1] Influence by the 'strenuous Whig' on such an ingrained Tory as Bute seems unlikely, but perhaps the belief then current that George Thomason had himself been a partisan of the King's cause made it possible to play on Bute's natural sympathies as a Stuart. In fact, Thomason was no royalist, but his political leanings were not widely known until much later.

The *Diary* entry for 4 April 1762 tells more of the story and brings it near its close:

M^r. Kent with me to acquaint me, that the Earl of Bute had purchased the whole collection of civil war tracts & Mss belonging to Miss Sisson of Ormond Street, noticed in my diary oct. 18, 1761, for £300., either for his Majesty or himself, with intention, as he believed, of bestowing them on the British Museum, that is the Public. The benefaction will be important, noble, by whom soe'er it is made, but especially from the King: M^r. Kent has promised, that he will speak to his friends to reppresent the matter in this light to the Earl of Bute, who there is I think no doubt, will then chearfully acquiesce in it.

As we know, events followed the predicted course. The King acquired the collection from Bute and presented it to the Museum, where it is such an extraordinary resource that it must now be protected from eager scholars who would wear it out through much consultation. There remains much we would be curious to know, but are unlikely to discover, concerning Hollis's undoubted involvement. Surely it was not confined to a couple of conversations with Mr Kent.

Throughout the *Diary* it is evident that Hollis kept in close touch with the market in coins and medals, antiquities, and most of all in books. For weeks and months at a time he made a daily round of the leading booksellers, he followed clues to out-of-the-way shops, and watched the

[1] *Memoirs*, pp. 121–2, 193–6, and Appendix LVIII, 717–18, reprinting a letter to the *London Chronicle* 20 Dec. 1752, no doubt written by Hollis, since it quotes the language of the *Diary*. See also Edwards, pp. 332–3; *Catalogue of the Pamphlets. . . Collected by George Thomason* (London 1908) I, pp. xviii–xix; Esdaile, pp. 181–3; Barker, pp. 64–6.

auction market as well. Among the books given to Harvard are several auction catalogues extensively marked. He appears to have attended sales in person whenever he could, putting in his own bids, and engaging trusted agents when he was unable to be present.

The resulting harvest provided bounty for individuals as well as institutions. Thus at the sale of Dr Joseph Letherland's library on 10 April 1765, he secured a miniature version of the Thomason Collection: lot 2861, 145 volumes of tracts of the Commonwealth period, knocked down at £10 1s.[1] He promptly sent the books to Mrs Macaulay to assist in the documentation of her *History of England*, which, as we know, he greatly admired. Similarly he constantly sought out appropriate tracts or collections to enrich the libraries of such friends and colleagues as Thomas Brand, Archdeacon Blackburne, Richard Baron, Caleb Fleming, John Free, and Theophilus Lindsey; and for those of them who were remote from London, he entered subscriptions for periodicals of suitably Old Whig tendencies.

Of course his institutional and personal benefactions extended to the New World, and we have already noted a few of them. He even tried to include the colony of Bermuda, but was disappointed to learn that no public library had as yet been established there. On the continent of North America he gave books to Yale, Princeton, Columbia, and the University of Pennsylvania, among others; not all of these institutions then bore the names by which we know them today. On one occasion his cousin Timothy tried to persuade him to become agent in Britain for the University of Pennsylvania, but he declined.[2]

His largest gifts and greatest efforts were reserved for the traditional recipient of Hollis family generosity, Harvard College. His earliest benefaction was a group of forty-four quarto volumes from the library of one of his heroes, Dr John Wallis, sent late in 1758. These were soon followed by the two-volume set of Milton's *Prose Works* bound by Richard Montagu, already described and pictured in chapter 2.[3] A

---

[1] Hollis's copy of the catalogues, with his markings, is at Harvard: B 1827.185*.

[2] *Diary* 26 November 1766.

[3] One possible survivor of the fire is *Speeches and Passages of this Great and Happy Parliament* (London 1641) (*EC65.G798P.B641ab), covering the period from 3 November 1640 to June 1641. Its title-page was inscribed by Hollis 'ut spargam' and 'Once belonging to the very eminent Dr. John Wallis.' John Langdon Sibley believed it had been part of a shipment received by the college in October 1764, but his evidence is not conclusive, and the question remains open. The volume is bound in sheep with non-emblematic decoration in a style found on other very early (pre-Montagu?) Hollis bindings; the binder has not been identified.

scattering of other books followed, but the pace of his giving did not increase until Harvard suffered its disastrous fire early in 1764. Long before that, the College's record-keeping had fallen into arrears, and some of his pre-fire gifts survived simply because their packing-cases remained unopened in storage, and the books had not yet found their way into the library.

In the face of this crisis, Hollis inserted advertisements in the London press urging others to help restore the Harvard collection, and engaged as well in personal solicitation. His own gifts to Harvard were not the random gleanings of the bookshops. They reveal Hollis as a purposeful and determined builder of collections, studying fields and making up lists of desiderata. The inscriptions they contain frequently reflect him as a shrewd buyer with his finger on the pulse of the market. He could draw on considerable funds, but he still objected strongly to an outside price. Two examples may suffice to show him as a keen and experienced competitor.

In the first of the three folio volumes of a set of Antonio Giggeo *Thesaurus linguae arabicae* (Milan 1632) he wrote:[1]

This is a fine Copy of a very scarce book. T·H has been particularly industrious in collecting Grammars & Lexicons of the Oriental, *Root* Languages, to send to Harvard College, in hope of forming by that Means, assisted by the Energy of the Leaders, always beneficent, a few PRIME Scholars, Honors to their Country & Lights to Mankind.

Two other works He wishes to have been able to send to that College.

'Gazophylacium Linguae Persarum', Amst. 1684, in folio.

'Meninski, Thesaurus Linguarum Orientalium' (containing the Arabic, Persic & Turkish Languages) Viennae, 1687. Tom. 4, in folio.

The first used to appear in the Catalogues, at a Guinea, 25ˢ. price. The last, even within these four Years, at about four Guineas. Now, when they appear, but that most rarely, ten, twenty Guineas is given for the former & *fifty* for the latter.

This Change has proceeded from the Gentlemen of our East India Factorys buying up all the Copies they can meet with of these Books; the more ingenious for themselves, artfully, to make presents to the Great Men & Literati of the East, to many of whom it seems, Books *of this Kind*, and the Gentlemen of Harvard will still rejoice at it as it may lead further, are peculiarly acceptable.

Lord Clive paid, it is said, Twenty Guineas for the 'Gazophylacium' just before he sailed from England. And Governor Van Sittart lately for his Brother, *Fifty* for the 'Meninski'.

There is no contending with Asiatics, Nabobbers!

[1] Harvard 3231.4F* v.1.

Despite these gloomy reflections in a key as familiar to book collectors today as in the eighteenth century, Hollis did indeed find and send to Harvard a good copy of the *Gazophylacium* of Angelo de St Joseph (Amsterdam 1684) with the following triumphant inscription:[1]

The Note in the *Giggeius* notwithstanding, I have since, most unexpectedly obtained this Book, &, as times go, at a cheap rate too, for 55 shillings.

It was sold in a public auction of no great Account; was probably unknown to the East India Buyers; and the Booksellers, who know I wish well to them & to the Press, Guard it North Americans! would not bid against me. T·H

Pall Mall, jan. 21, 67.

Like many a canny collector before and since, Hollis found it much to his advantage to be on good terms with the trade. Nevertheless he was prepared to do battle in the saleroom if necessary. In a copy of Christian Juncker's Latin biography of Martin Luther (Frankfurt 1699), which he bought and gave to Archdeacon Blackburne, he wrote, 'It is very rare; and, amid Friends & foes, like a River when opposed, was obtained by mining & strength'.[2] There was a touch of the poet or orator about him.

So much for Hollis's methods. As for his intellectual plan in assembling books for the edification of those he called 'the ingenuous youth of New England', no one should be surprised to find that it closely followed the outline laid down by Milton in *Of Education*, although the order of assembly and the weight given each topic did not exactly follow Milton's priority of subject, and some topics of special interest to Hollis appear rather more strongly than others, for example numismatics and classical archaeology. His command of the bibliography of philology is also rather surprising, as the examples already given indicate. Either he had excellent advice – a circumstance not recorded in the *Diary* – or he had taken great pains to inform himself.

Hollis could also be persuaded that Milton's scheme of priorities might be mistaken. Milton advocated the close study of Latin first, and Greek much later; but when Gregory Sharpe published *The Origin and Structure of the Greek Tongue* in 1767, Hollis wrote in the copy sent to Harvard that 'he humbly submits to the grave consideration of the very learned President, Professor & Teachers of that College, whether it

[1] Harvard 3261.8F*. Hollis never found the 1687 Meninski for the Harvard Library, which still must be content with a much later edition.
[2] Harvard *GC5.L9774.w699j; presented in 1979 by Dr Saul Jarcho.

might not be advisable, to adopt the idea thrown out in it, of teaching the Greek *before* the Latin Tongue, to all such Youths as *seek* and are intended *to be bred up Scholars*'.[1] James Harris's *Hermes*, also much admired by Hollis, may have helped to shape this opinion.

Again, he tried to influence the Harvard curriculum in three more-or-less similar inscriptions in books relating to agriculture and geology, objects also of Milton's concern. Typical of them is this in Francis Home's *The Principles of Agriculture* (London 1762): 'It is apprehended, the institution of a Professorship of Chemistry and Mineralogy at Cambridge in N. E. on the plan of those instituted in *Sueden* and some parts of Germany, which plan might easily be procured, would prove of more real, lasting benefit to North America, than all the vast wealth of a Nabob.'[2] (He seems to have been greatly impressed by nabobs, the oil sheiks of their day.)

Professor Caroline Robbins has surveyed the books given by Hollis to Harvard so well that I need not cover all of the same ground here.[3] Although many more Hollis gifts have been identified and recovered in the thirty-odd years since she published her work, the new discoveries do not materially change its outlines. One aspect of Hollis's collecting for Harvard is certainly worth reiterating, and that is involved with his connection with the neo-classical revival and its influence in North America. It appears in his emphasis on certain Greek and Latin texts, giving them equal weight with his favourite Commonwealth writers. Free men were to learn valuable lessons from the ancients. Thus in the copy sent to Harvard of *Observations on the Life of Cicero* (London 1733), where the anonymous author closes by remarking that Cicero's works are 'a strong Proof of how essential Freedom is to the Excellency of Writing', and that 'Force and Solidity of Reasoning, or a Sublime and Commanding Eloquence are inconsistent with Slavish Restraint, or Timorous Dependancy', Hollis wrote a characteristic exhortation in the margin: 'Mark well, O yet Ingenuous Youth, this Passage, & forsake not Liberty; nor the Assertor of it, who died gloriously in its behalf, the most accomplished, *excellent*, read his works, Marcus Tullius Cicero!!!'[4]

The lives of the heroes and martyrs of freedom always inspired Hollis, but never more strongly than as they were recounted by Plutarch, with his strong moral overtones. Hollis chose, it will be recalled, an epigraph from Plutarch's life of Brutus to be inscribed under his own portrait by

---

[1] Harvard x 27.20.83*.   [2] Harvard x 27.20.22*.   [3] See above, note 3 p. 29.
[4] Harvard *EC75.H7267.zz740m.

Cipriani. He sent editions of Plutarch in Latin and English to Harvard, and in the six-volume English edition of 1758, inscribed to the College on 1 November 1765, he wrote that it was 'a work, which at School he read avidly at times he might have slept, and to which he afterward became endebted for the honestest and finest dispositions of his Mind'.[1]

The volumes at Harvard are unusually worn and dog-eared, whether as inspirational reading for the 'ingenuous scholars' or as a crib in classical studies. But it cannot be denied that Plutarch's influence in the colonies was pervasive, and his models figured largely in thought and actions during the revolution and for many years after peace was concluded and the United States of America had achieved nationhood. Examples abound in the very names the patriots gave to their children, to say nothing of the title adopted by the organization of veterans of the war for independence: the Society of Cincinnati.

Rather than continue with such instances, it may be more profitable to follow one set of consequences of some importance that arose from the Hollis benefaction. In a favourite passage in *Areopagitica*, often marked by Hollis in the editions he gave away, Milton compares books to 'those fabulous dragon's teeth' which 'being sown up and down, may chance to spring up armed men'. In my first lecture I hinted that Hollis's liberty-texts, strikingly bound and prominently displayed in the Harvard College Library, provided a field liberally strewn with just such dragon's teeth, furnishing inspiration for at least some of the leaders in the break with the mother country that Hollis feared but did not live to see. We can trace with some degree of probability one train of events that began during his lifetime and continued long beyond it.

As we have seen, Hollis knew John Wilkes. On a first visit, 9 October 1759, he was not favourably impressed: 'A man of much low art, & a Wlpln [Walpolean] philosopher.' He cannot be said to have numbered him among his close friends, but he had more than a little sympathy for some of the causes that Wilkes espoused. A part of the repugnance that Hollis felt for the parliamentary system of his day was graphically illustrated in the prosecution of the notorious Number 45 of Wilkes's *North Briton* in 1763–64, ending with an illegal raid on Wilkes's house, his expulsion from the Commons, and his being declared an outlaw. Whatever personal sympathies may have been involved, such events could only alarm all who like Hollis profoundly believed in freedom of the press and the liberty of the subject.

---

[1] Harvard Gp 86.365* v.1.

Matters went even further in the second parliament of George III, when in 1768 the Middlesex voters three times elected Wilkes and three times saw him expelled. Crowds gathered in the streets to protest and had to be dispersed; one of Hollis's windows fronting on Pall Mall was broken during a mêlée, by accident and not through malice towards the tenant. More serious by far was the fatal shooting by militia in St George's Fields, Southwark, of a young man named William Allen, who, it was alleged, was not part of a mob but rather an innocent bystander. Claims were also made that the Riot Act had not been read before the troops opened fire. Indignation ran high. One of Hollis's friends among the dissenting clergy, the Reverend John Free, preached a powerful sermon in which he attacked the government as responsible for the atrocity. A year later Free preached an equally powerful sermon on the anniversary of Allen's death.

Hollis welcomed Free's sermons and began assembling as full a set as possible of all of his writings, intended to be sent to Harvard. But, as we have seen, he took the unusual step of having Free's first sermon, *England's Warning Piece*, and its anniversary companion, bound together in black leather with mourning endpapers and a black ribbon marker. (The rest of the set of Free's works is bound in ordinary brown calf.) He sent this volume to the Harvard College Library, where it was received on 18 August 1769. It must have presented a striking contrast to the red and green morocco and shining calf in the Hollis alcoves.[1]

On 5 March 1770 occurred the event known as the Boston Massacre, in its origin quite different from the Wilkes Riots and the Massacre of St George's Fields, but at least with superficial parallels. Local citizens gathered to protest and to taunt the British troops quartered in the town, pelting them with snowballs and stones; teased beyond endurance, the soldiers fired without orders, and five civilians lay dead or dying.

At a meeting of the freeholders and inhabitants of Boston shortly thereafter, James Bowdoin, Dr Joseph Warren, and Samuel Pemberton were appointed a committee to compile and publish the facts in the case. All three were respected citizens and one of them, Bowdoin, was a professed admirer of Hollis, and had written a lengthy poem hailing Hollis and Jonathan Mayhew as examples of patriotism and lovers of freedom.[2] The committee reported publicly in the well-known pamph-

---

[1] Harvard *EC75.F8754.768ec. In the *Diary* 8 June 1769, Hollis tells of 'preparing' copies of Free's *Anniversary Sermon* for distribution.

[2] The poem is printed in W. H. Bond 'Letters from Thomas Hollis of Lincoln's Inn to Andrew Eliot' *Proceedings of the Massachusetts Historical Society* 99 (1988), pp. 126–8.

let, *A Short Narrative of the Horrid Massacre* (Boston 1770), which was not reticent about putting its case on the very title-page.

Word of the events of 5 March had reached Hollis in London by 28 April, when he saw and obtained leave to copy a 'curious letter' about the affair which had been received at the bookshop of Edward and Charles Dilly. Two days later the *Diary* notes a long conversation with the Reverend Caleb Fleming 'on the late Slaughter at Boston in N. E. & the sad consequences which will probably result to the whole British Empire, if Government shall attempt vigorous measures with the People of N[orth]. A[merica].!' In succeeding weeks Hollis paid repeatedly to have minatory advertisements printed in the public journals, drawing one of them from the motto on a Dutch medal (deriving ultimately from Alciati's *Emblems*), 'FRANGIMVR SI COLLIDIMVR', which reminded readers of the picture usually accompanying it: two earthenware vessels jostling against one another as they are carried down a turbulent stream. He purchased quantities of the London reprint of the *Short Narrative* for broadcast distribution, and ordered some of them to be bound in black on the pattern of Free's sermons on the killing of William Allen. As noted earlier, he placed a copy of the Boston edition so bound in the library of Christ's College.

Somewhat to his surprise, but quite possibly because Free's black book on the Wilkes affair was so conspicuous on Harvard's shelves (and also because of much sympathetic correspondence between Hollis and Andrew Eliot on the deplorable state of colonial relations, and numerous interviews with visiting New Englanders), Hollis now received a direct appeal from the New World. On 18 June 1770 he recorded:

Received a packet from N. E. by M[r]. Lever of the N[ew]. E[ngland]. C[offee]. H[ouse].[1] the seals of which seemed rather to have been tampered with. It contained a Vote of the Freeholders & other Inhabitants of the Town of Boston, in public Town meeting assembled, on thursday, march 22, 70, directing that 'the Hon. James Bowdoin, D[r]. Joseph Warren, and Samuel Pemberton Esq., a Committee appointed march 13, to make representation of the late horrid Massacre in Boston by the Soldiery, be desired to transmit by Packet, to Thomas Hollis Esq. F. R. S. a printed copy of such representation.' It contained, likewise, a letter to T·H from that Committee, requesting on behalf of the Town of Boston, '*the favor of HIS interposition & influence!* that the Troops in the Province of

---

[1] Hollis, suspecting that his mail was likely to be opened by government agents, had earlier arranged for Thomas Lever's coffee house behind the Royal Exchange to serve as a cover address. On other occasions he used his binder, John Shove, as a cover address.

Massachusetts-Bay might be withdrawn from it, & the loyal subjects of the Town & Province not again be distressed by them.

Answered it at once.

'Gentlemen,

The Packet, with a *duplicate* letter, dated march 23, 1770, was received this day.

I shall be proud, at all times, to shew respect to the People of the Town of Boston and Province of Massachusetts, believing them to be a virtuous, loyal, and magnanimous People. But, so ordinary a Person am I, and so very a Whig, that I do not apprehend I can be of other use to them, than to send them a few books, occasionally, for their College. I have the honor to be, Gentlemen,

Your most humble servant

T·H'

That can hardly have been the response for which the Bostonians were hoping, though scarcely surprising in view of Hollis's earlier rebuff by the Prime Minister. And Hollis had other ways of helping. He went about it in his usual private fashion. On 20 June he noted in his *Diary*:

Went by water from Hungerford to the three cranes. Breakfasted at the N. E. C. H. With Mess. Dilly. Gave them three guineas to reprint here, the ten last pages of the 'Narrative of the horrid Massacre in Boston, perpetrated in the evening of the fifth day of march 1770', which pages were in the copy of the Narrative sent to me by vote of the Town of Boston, but were not in the copies of it first sent to England and other parts – Service of this sort is the best, it is apprehended, which I can render to the worthy, and now, alas, distressed People of Boston – to cause their sentiments to be made known on this side the water, on points of highest consequence to both of Us.

The story continues, and here I am much indebted to the research of the late Professor Chester Noyes Greenough, first published in 1918.[1]

One of the most unpopular tasks ever undertaken by John Adams, later second President of the United States, was the successful defence of Captain Thomas Preston, who had commanded the British troops involved in the Massacre. Near the close of his courtroom speech, delivered in 1770, Adams employed phrases that would have quite a different application later:

To use the words of a great and worthy man, a patriot and a hero, an enlightened friend to mankind, and a martyr to liberty – I mean Algernon Sidney – who from his earliest infancy sought a tranquil retirement under the shadow of the tree of liberty, with his tongue, his pen, and his sword.

Manus haec, inimica tyrannis,

Ense petit placidam sub libertate quietem.

---

[1] 'Algernon Sidney and the Motto of the Commonwealth of Massachusetts' *Proceedings of the Massachusetts Historical Society* 51 (1918), pp. 259–82; reprinted in Greenough's *Collected Studies* ([Cambridge, Mass.] 1940), pp. 68–88.

Although the parallel between Algernon Sidney and Captain Preston is far from clear, the quotation was emotionally and rhetorically effective. It does not seem to have a classical source. Without much question, Adams found it through the intermediacy of Thomas Hollis, who in turn had discovered it in an anecdote about Sidney in the preface to a favourite book by Lord Molesworth, the *Short Account of Denmark*.

Briefly, the story tells how, during an official embassy to Sweden and Denmark in 1659, Algernon Sidney gave offence to royal personages by writing those Latin words in the visitors' album at the University in Copenhagen. There is reason to believe that the phrase was original with Sidney. It is certainly consonant with his life and with the arguments in his *Discourses Concerning Government*, which in the end helped bring him to the block in 1683, even though he had earlier refused to have anything to do with the proceedings that had brought Charles I to the same fate.

Hollis caused the anecdote and motto to be cut at the foot of the woodcut portrait of Sidney by John Baptist Jackson referred to earlier. Copies of this print were sent to New England in 1758 along with the edition of Sidney's *Discourses* of 1751.

Four years later Hollis commissioned Cipriani to draw, and James Basire to engrave, another portrait of Sidney. Once more the anecdote and its motto were prominently displayed; once more copies went to New England, some of them in 1763 as frontispiece to a new edition of the *Discourses*, anonymously edited by Hollis himself. He also wrote the biographical introduction in which the anecdote was told yet again.

When Hollis had copies of another canonical work, Locke's *Letters Concerning Toleration* (1765) bound for distribution, he directed that the words 'PLACIDAM SVB LIBERTATE QVIETEM' should be lettered in gold on the back cover of a number of copies. Such a copy went to Harvard, another is at Christ's College, and another, now in the Massachusetts Historical Society, was inscribed by Hollis to the Bostonian, James Otis, as 'an Assertor of Liberty, civil and religious'.[1]

We can scarcely doubt where John Adams found the striking phrase; indeed, he could hardly have avoided seeing it. But its use was not, and even now is not, at an end.

In 1775, when the government of the Massachusetts Bay Colony was being reorganized at Watertown, the next town to Cambridge, its Executive Council directed a committee to devise a seal for the colony.

---

[1] Another such copy, originally presented to the Duke of Newcastle, is in the possession of the author. Some copies, otherwise identical, bear the Libertas emblem instead of the motto.

The committee was headed by John Winthrop and James Otis, son of the James Otis to whom Hollis had given the copy of Locke's *Letters Concerning Toleration*.

Their first suggestion was an American Indian holding a tomahawk in one hand and a liberty-cap in the other, with the motto 'Petit sub libertate quietem', but the Council quickly changed the figure to 'an English American, holding a Sword in the Right Hand, and Magna Charta in the Left Hand', and the House determined that the motto should be enlarged to read 'Ense petit placidam sub libertate quietem', all of which was adopted. Otis, of course, had the motto ready to hand, but others surely were familiar with it.

Sidney's Latin tag made its official debut on 18 August on the forty-shilling banknote engraved by Paul Revere.[1] It remains the official motto of the Commonwealth of Massachusetts to this day, and there is probably a further distant reflection of Thomas Hollis in the fact that Massachusetts is one of the few regional governments in the United States to call itself a Commonwealth rather than a State. One may doubt that many modern legislators think of it as other than a possibly grander word than 'State', or that they have more than a hazy notion of what the motto signifies or where it came from. They are far too busy devising new methods of taxation, which started the trouble in the first place.

And so Hollis's books, sent to Harvard College and to individual colonists, proved to be dragon's teeth indeed, and sprang up armed men. 'For books are not absolutely dead things, but do contain a potency of life in them to be as active as that soul was whose progeny they are; nay, they do preserve as in a vial the purest efficacy of that living intellect that bred them. . . embalmed and treasured up on purpose to a life beyond life.' The books that Thomas Hollis selected and bound so carefully more than two centuries ago are ready on the shelves today and are still consulted, and no one can tell when they may next serve a great purpose, or what that purpose may be. Meanwhile they are as permanent as any human testimony can be of what one man can do 'By deeds of peace'.

---

[1] See Clarence S. Brigham *Paul Revere's Engravings* (New York 1969), plates 75 and 76.

Index

Bloesch, Hans, 'Ein Englischer
 Gönner der Berner
 Stadtbibliothek', 56 n.1
Boccaccio, Giovanni, *Decamerone*, ed.
 Vincenzio Martinelli, 93, 96, 99
Bohun, William, 8
Bond, W. H., 'Assertor of Liberty', 32
 n.2; 'Letters from Thomas Hollis
 . . . to Andrew Eliot', 119 n.2;
 'Thomas Hollis and Samuel
 Johnson', 2 n.2
Book Collector, 56 n.1
Bosco, Domenico and Saverio,
 fencing-masters, 14 n.3
Boscovic, Rudyer Josip, *De solis ac
 lunae defectibus libri v*, 93
Boston, Mass., 29
Boston Massacre, 39 n.2, 118–21
Boston Tea Party, 33
Boswell, James, 1, 35; *Account of
 Corsica*, 2, 63–4; *Boswell with
 Rousseau and Voltaire 1764*, 34;
 *Essays in Favour of the Brave
 Corsicans*, 64; imitations of Hollis
 tools, 63–4; *Journal 1779–1781*, 1
 n. 1; *Life of Johnson*, 1, 34; *Private
 Papers*, 1 n.1
Bowdoin, James, 118–19; poem on
 Hollis and Mayhew, 118; *Short
 Narrative of the Horrid Massacre*, 39
 n.2, 118–20
Bowyer, William, 84–5, 87, 96; ed.
 Greek New Testament, 84–5;
 presentation inscription, 85 n.1
Brand, Thomas, *see* Hollis, Thomas
 Brand
Brander, Gustavus, 81
Brattle, William, 4
Brigham, Clarence S., *Paul Revere's
 Engravings*, 122 n.1
Britannia victrix, 81–2
British Library, 111 n.2, 112 n.1; *see
 also* British Museum
British Museum, 60, 110–12;
 Additional MSS, 7 n.2, 10 n.2,
 15 n.1–2; Costa gift, 111;
 Grenville Collection, 28 n.1;
 Thomason Tracts, 111–13,
 Catalogue, 112 n.1; Trustees reject
 anti-Jesuit print, 110

Brown, John, *An Estimate of the Times*,
 26
Brown, Laurence, *Catalogue of British
 Historical Medals*, 49 n.1
Brutus, Lucius Junius, 74
Brutus, Marcus, 20, 23, 33, 64, 99,
 116
Buonarroti, Filippo, *Osservazioni sopra
 alcuni frammenti*, 69–71
Burnet, Thomas, *De statu mortuorum*,
 70 n.1
Burrow, J. W., *A Liberal Descent*, 16
Bute, 3rd Earl of, *see* Stuart, John

Cadell, Thomas, 87, 100
Cambridge, Mass., 5, 121
Cambridge University Library, 9 n.2
Canada, Roman Catholic bishop in,
 19
Canaletto, Antonio Canale, called,
 14, 20 n.2, 24, 81
carbon prints, *see* smoke prints
Carter, Elizabeth, 1–2, 6, 12 n.4
Carthage, coin, 71 n.2
Castello, Gabriele Lancilotto, Prince
 of Torremuzza, 12, 108
Castor and Pollux, 64
Catania, Sicily, monastery, 10, 12
Celsus, *De arte medici libri octo*, 40 n.2
Chamberlayne, John, ed. *Oratio
 Dominica*, 8 n.1
Chambers, Sir William, 108
Charles I, King, 34, 65, 67, 69, 82,
 121
Charles II, King, 23, 73; collection of
 Hebrew books, 111
Chatham, Earl of, *see* Pitt, William
Cheere, Sir Henry, 80 n.2
chemistry, study advocated, 113
Christie's, 14 n.1
Christ's College, Cambridge, 39 n.2,
 46 n.1, 109–10, 119, 121
church bells, 18
Church of England, 6, 85
Churchill, Mrs Lawrence, 55 n.1
Cicero, Marcus Tullius, 116
Cipriani, Giovanni Battista, 18, 20,
 23–5, 27, 80 n.2, 107; designs for
 tools, 49–52, 54–77; designs for
 Wedgwood Etruscan ware, 107;

Cipriani, Giovanni Battista (*cont.*)
drawings, xvi; 'Britannia victrix',
67–8; 'Milton victorious over
Salmasius', 82; 'O fair Britannia
hail', 67; portrait of Algernon
Sidney, 82, 121; portrait of
Boccaccio, 93, 96; portrait of
Hollis, 23–5, 116–17; portrait of
Locke, 93; 'View of the
Committee Room', Marine
Society, 83
Clayton, Robert, Bishop, *The Bishop of
Clogher's Speech*, 52
Clive, Robert, Baron Clive, 114
Cobham Warehouse, Lyme, 31
Cock of Gaul, 62
Cock of Portugal, 62
Columbia University, 113
Committee for the Relief of French
Prisoners, 24; *Proceedings*, 66–7,
93–4
Commodus, 75
Commonwealth, 28, 80, 111–12, 116
Constable, W. G., *Canaletto*, 14 n.1;
Richard Wilson, 12 n.3
Cooper, Alexander, portrait of
Cromwell, 110
Copenhagen, 108; University, 121
Corscombe, Dorset, 8 n.1, 10, 18, 33
Costa, Solomon da, gift to the British
Museum, 111
Coste, Pierre, 110
Cosway, Richard, 80 n.2
Cromwell, Oliver, 9 n.2, 28; portrait
by Cooper, 110
Cupid, 70–1

Davies, Thomas, 87
Davis, Lockyer, 87
Declaration of Independence, 28
Della Terza, Mollie, 20 n.1
Denmark, 121
Dilly, Charles and Edmund, 87, 99,
119
Dioscuri, 64
Disney, Edgar Norton, sale (1950), 12
n.3
Disney, John, 44–5, 55, 86; *Memoirs of
Thomas Brand-Hollis*, 9 n.1, 15;
sale (1817), 7 n.1, 35 and n.3

Dr Williams's Library, 110
Dodsley, James, 87
Dodsley, Robert, 86–7, 93 n.1
Dodsworth, British consul at Malta,
14
Dorset, Hollis farms in, 6, 10–11, 19,
31, 81 n.3, 107; names of farms,
32; County Archives, 32 n.2
Doyley, John, survey of Hollis farms,
32 n.2
Dudley, Joseph, 3–4
Dulwich Gallery, 14 n.1

East India Company, 99, 114–15
Eck, Reimer, 71 n.1
Edward VI, King, autograph MS,
111
Edwards, Edward, *Lives of the Founders
of the British Museum*, 111 n.2, 112
n.1
Egmont, Justus ab, portrait of
Algernon Sidney, 82
Eimer, Christopher, *British
Commemorative Medals*, 67 n.1
Eliot, Andrew, 18–19, 26 n.2, 27–8,
60–1, 97–8, 118 n.2, 119
Eliot, John, 98
Elizabeth I, Queen, 84
Engell, James, ed. *Johnson and His Age*,
2 n.2
Ense petit . . ., see *Placidam sub libertate
quietem*
epigraphy, 88–9
Erasmus, *Complaint of Peace*, tr.
Vicesimus Knox, 55 n.2; *Epistolae*
presented by William Bowyer, 85
n.1
Eschler, Margaret, 59 n.2, 70 n.1
Esdaile, Arundel, *The British Museum*
111 n.2, 112 n.1
Etruscan ware, 107
Evelyn, John, 111

Fabretti, Raphael, *Inscriptionum
antiquarum . . . explicatio*, 88
Fairbairn, James, *Fairbairn's Book of
Crests*, 44 n.1
Falstaff, 87
Fane, John, 7th Earl of Westmorland,
11

Links, Joseph G., *Canaletto and His Patrons*, 14 n.1
Linnaeus, Carl, 108
Locke, John, 6, 45, 108; *Commonplace Book*, 84; *Letters Concerning Toleration* (1765), 27 n.1, 93, 121–2; portrait of, 82, 93; *Two Treatises of Government* (1690), 39 n.1; *Two Treatises of Government* (1698), annotated by Locke and Pierre Coste, 110; *Two Treatises of Government* (1764), 93
London Chronicle, 29 n.2, 83, 85, 88, 97 n.2, 112 n.1
Louisbourg, medal on capture of, 52
Low Countries, 109
Lowth, Robert, Bishop, 96
Lucan, Strawberry Hill ed., 27 n.1
Luckhurst, Kenneth W., *see* Hudson, Derek
Ludlow, Edmund, portrait of, 82
Luther, Martin, 115
Lyme Regis, 8 n.1, 10–11, 18, 31

Maber, Peter, 10–11
Macardell, James, 80 n.2, 81
Macaulay, Catherine Sawbridge, 108; *History of England*, 99–100, 113; *Loose Remarks on . . . Hobbes*, 99, 101–2; portrait of, 82
McKitterick, David, 64 n.1
Magdalen Hospital, 24
Maggs Brothers Ltd, *Bookbindings in the British Isles*, 46 n.1
Major, Thomas, 79, 80 n.1
Malta, 97
marbled paper, Dutch style, 37–8; French style, 37–8
Marine Society, 24, 83
Martin, Benjamin, 14
Martin (father and son), fencing-masters, 23
Martinelli, Vincenzio, ed. Boccaccio, *Decamerone*, 93, 96, 99
Marvell, Andrew, 68; portrait of, 82; *Works*, 71
Mason, William, 27
Massachusetts, Commonwealth of, motto, 82, 120 n.1, 122

Massachusetts Bay Colony, charter, 3–4; Executive Committee, 121; House of Representatives, 97; seal, 121–2
Massachusetts Historical Society, 18 n.1, 28 n.1, 121
Massacre in St George's Fields, 39 n.2, 118
Mather, Increase, 3–4
Matthewman, John, binder, 36–7, 39, 41–2, 46, 49, 52–5, 97, 110; destruction of his shop by fire, 53
Maty, Matthew, 108
Mauduit, Israel, 27
Mauduit, Jasper, 27
Mayhew, Jonathan, 26 n.2, 27, 33, 60–1, 118; portrait of, 82; sermons on the taking of Quebec, 85
Medusa, 65–7
Meerman, Gerard, *Origines typographiae*, 88
Meninski, François, *Thesaurus linguarum orientalium*, 114–15
Mercer, Malcolm, 'The Hollis Educational Trust', 5 n.1
Mercury, *see* Hermes
Messala, 23
Middlesex electors, 118
Millar, Andrew, 26, 85–7, 93, 96–7, 107
Milton, John, 2, 33, 45, 67–9, 83, 108–9; *Areopagitica*, 88, 117, 122; bed given to Akenside, 26; *Cosmus*, 26; *Eikonoklastes*, 26, 46–7; motto from *Paradise Regained*, xv, 60, 122; *Of Education*, 7–8, 10–11, 115; 'On the Late Massacre in Piemont', 9 n.2; *Paradise Lost*, 26, 109; *Paradise Regained*, 26, 33; *Poems*, 109; portraits of, 82; *Prose Works*, ed. Richard Baron (1753–56), 34, 46–8, 68, 70, 76, 82 n.2, 113; *Prose Works*, ed. Richard Baron, abandoned (1767), 87; *Samson Agonistes*, 26; second sonnet to Cyriack Skinner, 33; sonnets, 26
mineralogy, study advocated, 116
Mitten, David Gordon, 57, 59 n.5

For EU product safety concerns, contact us at Calle de José Abascal, 56–1°,
28003 Madrid, Spain or eugpsr@cambridge.org.

www.ingramcontent.com/pod-product-compliance
Ingram Content Group UK Ltd.
Pitfield, Milton Keynes, MK11 3LW, UK
UKHW030902150625
459647UK00021B/2663